INDEPENDENT AND UNOFFICIAL
THE BEST
ROBLOX
GAMES
EVER!

Published in 2020 by Mortimer Children's Books Limited, an imprint of
the Welbeck Publishing Group, 20 Mortimer Street, London W1T 3JW

Text, design and illustration © Welbeck Publishing Limited 2020

ISBN: 978 1 83935 015 3

Printed in Dongguan, China

3 5 7 9 10 8 6 4 2

Author: Kevin Pettman
Layout and design: Dynamo Ltd.
Design Manager: Sam James
Editorial Manager: Joff Brown
Production: Sarah Cook

INDEPENDENT AND UNOFFICIAL

THE BEST
ROBLOX
GAMES
EVER!

MORTIMER

CONTENTS

GAME ON!

Welcome to the fun, awesome and exciting world of ROBLOX! You're about to explore over 100 incredible games and discover epic tips, guides, facts and stats. So, enjoy the adventure!

TAKE CONTROL!

Get to know all about your awesome avatar character and master the controls, commands and options in the ROBLOX universe...

After downloading ROBLOX onto a tablet, smartphone, computer or Xbox console and setting up your account, the next step is to create your avatar (character) to play as in any of the thousands of ROBLOX games.

From the Avatar Shop you have heaps of options to add and change, such as coloured shirts, pants, hairstyles and hats. Getting your own personal look is a big part of the game!

ROBLOX FASHION

Clothing and accessories for avatars can be paid for with ROBUX (the in-game currency in ROBLOX), but can also be picked up for free!

In the Catalog section, make sure you list from 'Low to High' price to show all of the free things at the top. This applies for all clothing, and bundles – where you get a complete outfit – heads, faces and accessories.

Themed outfits and avatars often appear in the Avatar Shop, ranging from big brands and events such as Marvel and Star Wars movies, to famous TV shows like Doctor Who. There have also been official sport linkups with the NFL, Barcelona FC and Liverpool FC. Be quick to get them, though, as they only appear for a limited time!

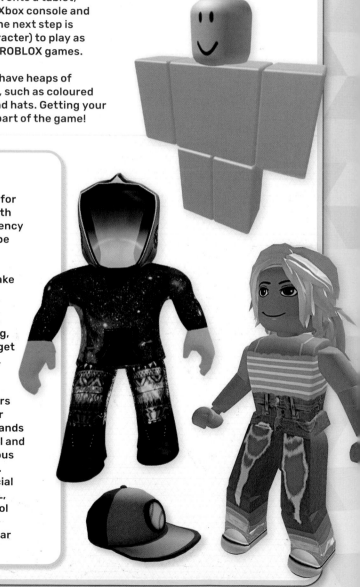

CONTROL OPTIONS

Your control options for your avatar depend on the platform you play on. To check exactly what these are, choose the menu button (it's represented by three horizontal lines) and then the help tab. This shows you how to make character and camera movements, as well as other helpful instructions.

Xbox One console players can access their control configurations by clicking the menu button on their controller. Go to the settings option by pressing the left thumbstick up, then clicking right bumper (RB) for the help tab.

The settings option (represented by a white cog symbol) also allows players to adjust things such as graphics quality and mode, mouse sensitivity and volume. The navigation bar is a helpful way to quickly access info for your avatar and general ROBLOX play. It appears on the left side of your screen and opens options such as Profile, Friends, Avatar and Inventory.

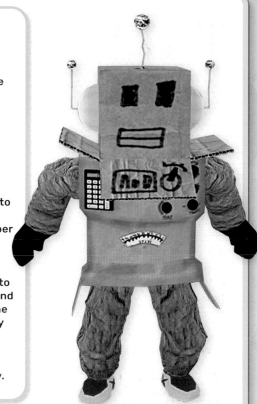

- DID YOU KNOW? -

The create tab takes you to the Studio section, which is where you can start creating and building your very own ROBLOX games!

STAYING SAFE

ROBLOX is a wonderful world of games and fun to enjoy with friends and communities, and there are lots of ways to make sure that everyone stays safe online.

PERSONAL INFO

Personal information including your name, address or school should not be revealed in ROBLOX. It is important that your account names do not reflect those in real life. Never give away personal information, including email addresses or phone numbers, and never share any passwords.

CHAT SETTINGS

Chatting with other players is possible through typing messages that appear on the screen. All ROBLOX chat is filtered carefully so that inappropriate things cannot be said. Players aged 12 and under have stricter controls and filters than those aged 13 and above.

ROBUX

Any links, games or users that promise to give you free ROBUX should not be clicked on or joined. ROBUX is only available through the official ROBLOX company and always has to be paid for, either as a single payment or as part of an ongoing membership.

Buy Robux	Subscribe and get more!
◎ 400	◎ 450/month
◎ 800	◎ 1,000/month
◎ 1,700	◎ 2,200/month

Value Packs

◎ 4,500	
◎ 10,000	

REPORT IT

If something happens in a game that upsets or worries you, you should tell a parent or guardian. You can report bad behaviour directly to ROBLOX. To do this, click on the menu button and use the Report flag by a user's name or the Report tab above it. Games and catalog and library items can also be reported if they break ROBLOX rules.

SENSIBLE SETTINGS

When setting up accounts with their children, parents can place limits and restrictions on what they can do. The account settings section allows this and options can be set on what contact a user can have with others, as well as the types of games available to them.

- DID YOU KNOW? -

Parents can add an account PIN to lock a user's settings and protect things like privacy settings and password. The '2-step verification' feature adds an extra security layer by sending a code to the person in charge of the account.

SOCIAL SHARING

Game developers can share their social media links with the people who play their games, and this is an option available in the games area of the homepage. Developers can share up to three social media links in game descriptions, including YouTube and Twitch. Social media links can only be seen by accounts that are aged 13 years or older.

TOP TIPS!

Whether you're a 'newb' to the land of **ROBLOX** or an experienced pro player, these handy hints will help your gameplay and let you have even more fun.

GAME GREATS

1 Choosing what game to play can seem troublesome because there are SOOOO many options in the Games section! Use Popular, Top Rated and Featured rankings to help you decide what to play, and also the percentage ratings and concurrent figures under the game title to see how popular they are. The search bar lets you type in the keywords if you want to unearth a great game you may have missed.

BE A LEADER

2 The in-game leaderboard is often a great tool to check out info, such as who else is playing in your game, the scores and status icons. These icons can display details such as who your friends are, any premium members and ROBLOX admins.

PRACTICE MAKES PERFECT

3 It's true – the more you play ROBLOX games and become familiar with the functions, the better you'll be and the more fun you'll have! Just make sure you play in the ROBLOX world for a healthy amount of time agreed between you and your parents or guardians.

EPIC EVENTS

4 Through the menu option on the ROBLOX homepage, the Events section can be seen at the bottom. This features links to things like video games, movies and holiday seasons with exclusive content, games, items and more. In March 2020, the BLOXYS awards event was heavily featured here!

EVENTS

MAGIC MEMORIES

5 From the homepage menu button, the record button lets you do exactly that – record a ROBLOX moment as a video so that you can watch it again. Click the record tab and follow the instructions. You have the option to take screenshots of your in-game moments.

RECORD

TALK TIME

6 A big part of ROBLOX is being able to type messages or chat through a headset to other players. This can really help a group-based game! It lets you communicate safely with your friends and fellow players and have an enjoyable time. Turn to pages 10-11 for tips on online safety.

LET'S PLAY A GAME!

MAKE A MOVE

7 As well as creating your avatar in either R6, R15 or Rthro proportions to give yourself a look you like, you can often bust out a sick series of dances! Called Emotes, they are instructions you can give your character to do a slick – or silly – dance routine. Some games even have special buttons you can press to perform a rockin' routine!

- DID YOU KNOW? -

Players can reset their avatar during a game and begin again at a spawn point. From the menu, just select the **Reset Character** option.

AWARD WINNING GAMES

The Bloxy Awards is the biggest event of the year! It's where they give out prizes to the stars of the ROBLOX world.

HALL OF FAME

The awards began as a celebration of video creators and animators. It now includes artists and social media influencers, too. There are over 20 awards each year, with hundreds of thousands of votes and millions watching via live streams around the world!

MOBILE GAME OF THE YEAR

101

Welcome To Bloxburg
by **Coeptus**

👍 **RATING: 90%**

VISITS:	1.8B+
CREATED:	4/11/2014
GENRE:	Town & City

BEST SLEEPER HIT

100

ADVENTURE UP!
by **Ready, set, play!**

👍 **RATING: 87%**

VISITS	27M+
CREATED	19/5/2019
GENRE	RPG

BEST SHOWCASE

99

Toyokawa Inari Shrine
by **nezko**

👍 **RATING: 86%**

VISITS	1.2M+
CREATED	9/5/2019
GENRE	All Genres

BEST BREAKOUT GAME

98

Ninja Legends
by **Scriptbloxian Studios**

👍 **RATING: 60%**

VISITS	800M+
CREATED	22/9/2019
GENRE	Adventure

BEST LOBBY

97

RUMBLE QUEST
by **Rumble Studios**

👍 **RATING: 87%**

VISITS	152M+
CREATED	15/11/2019
GENRE	All Genres

BEST GAME UPDATE

96

ADOPT ME
by **DreamCraft**

👍 **RATING: 92%**

VISITS	5B+
CREATED	14/7/2017
GENRE	RPG

GAME OF THE YEAR

95

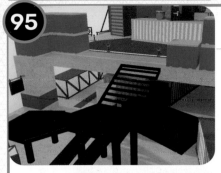

ARSENAL
by ROLVe Community

Arsenal is a multi-winning Bloxy game. In 2020 it picked up the big prize of Game of the Year. It was up against the mighty titles of Adopt Me, Royale High, Mad City and Welcome to Bloxburg. Arsenal's slick style and all-action adventures really caught the imagination. It's a top-class First Person Shooter and the weapons and customizable content keeps gamers coming back for more!

QUICK STATS

👍 BEST GAMES RATING: **92%**

VISITS:	CREATED:	GENRE:
670M+	18/8/2015	FPS

XBOX GAME OF THE YEAR

94

MURDER MYSTERY 2
by Nikilis

Facing ROBLOX High School 2 and Mad City for the prize, MM2 swept to success and Xbox players can't get enough of it! The innocents and the sheriff take on the murderer around a scary location, with chasing and hiding as much a part as battling with weapons. It takes teamwork and tactics to get the better of the baddie and coins and XP boosts are the rewards on offer.

QUICK STATS

👍 BEST GAMES RATING: **91%**

VISITS:	CREATED:	GENRE:
2.4B+	18/1/2014	Horror

TOWN AND CITY

ROBLOX games are sorted into lots of genres, and Town and City is one of the biggest and best! Turn over to check out a stack of the top titles in this class, featuring everything from racecars to robbers and urban heroes to high school mayhem. If you love adventures, missions, minigames, upgrades and loads more, then take a tour through the T&C landscape!

RATING REVALED

There are over 100 ROBLOX games in this book and each one has been specially rated for you! The higher the rating, the better the game is. It is an overall rating based on scores such as fun, difficulty, appearance and individuality. Try them all for yourself and see which ones you like best of all.

93 MAD CITY

by Schwifty Studios

Weekly challenges, new weapons, heists and fast-paced action – Mad City has it all! Now with a few years of development behind it and closing in on 1 billion visits over this time, this Town and City trailblazer is super slick looking and totally addictive.

The game begins by offering users a choice between joining the Police, Heroes or Prisoner outfits. They are all as fun as each other and each spawn (at the start) in a different location. But choosing to be a cop gives you the option of purchasing body armour from the Police base straight away... for a cool 6,000 Robux, though! Baddies can also pick up this extra-protective suit to boost health by 50 and gain a big advantage.

QUICK STATS

BEST GAMES
RATING: 88%

VISITS: 950M+

CREATED: 3/12/2017

GENRE: Town & City

- DID YOU KNOW? -

In a season 5 mini update, a police officer's dog needed a whistle to be blown so that it would pursue and slow down a criminal!

Mad City's mission is to complete tasks in your chosen outfit (such as arresting criminals, robbing and escaping) and earning benefits from this. Keep an eye on your XP level after you achieve these as it'll increase, and you can then progress to a higher rank. There's always talk among ROBLOXIANS about whether Mad City or the Jailbreak game is better. They are very similar, but Mad City feels a bit older in gameplay style and has a bigger map.

Being a Hero is always a popular choice, not least because having a power such as Hotrod (speed), Inferno (fireball) and Proton (laser beam) is a real game changer in the city! Don't forget to have a quick weight lifting session in the superhero lobby and earn a quick XP boost... and show off your Hero-sized muscles, too!

The developers at Schwifty Studios are very good at keeping the game fresh and appealing, so there are always reasons to head back to Mad City. This often means updating the scenery and locations (in spring 2020 the airport had a new look after being the same since season 1!) and dropping in to check out new rewards, weapons and skins. Season 5 brought in new player homes, which was pretty epic!

BETTER GET OUT OF HERE!

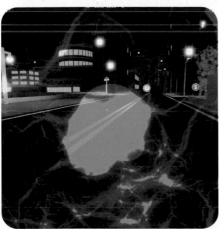

92 JAILBREAK

Are you going to be on the good team or the bad team? Fight for justice or take and plunder what you can? These are the choices at the start of Jailbreak, the legendary ROBLOX Town and City title packed with drama, options and a heavy selection of the Role Playing Game (RPG) genre too.

by Badimo

QUICK STATS

👍 BEST GAMES **RATING: 89%**

VISITS: 3.4B+

CREATED: 6/1/2017

GENRE: Town & City

Choose to start with the Police and you have the option of four items – pistol, taser, handcuffs and spike trap. Inside the base the action begins, with characters on the run and crims to catch. Keep an eye on your daily missions and status bar (to see things like the number of people you need to arrest), and remember that cop cars are a little faster than criminal vehicles, which helps in road rumbles with robbers!

Being a crim from the off means you need to be sneaky. Pickpocket keycards to escape the base and begin your rampage at banks in the city! Tunnels also help you bust out of the compound, plus simple crouching can help you get under wired fencing. Work as a team to breach the security, while punching wall pads to open gates is a simple but effective measure. Be smart and don't overthink it – if you can't bash open the fence while driving a car, simply

LET'S GO FOR A RIDE!

NOW'S MY CHANCE!

LOCKED AND LOADED!

standing on top of the vehicle and jumping the barrier will work!

A cool feature of Jailbreak is being able to play music on the stereo in any vehicle, which gives those high-speed dashes through the streets and high-flying aerial copper chopper sweeps even more entertainment! It'll cost 250 Robux, but if you are in the mood for a musical treat, give it a go!

Had enough of being a police officer or a crim while you're mid-game? No problem, as Jailbreak has an option to switch sides in an instant. Hit the orange-blue stick figure icon on the left of the screen in computer platforms, and you can confirm you're jumping to the other team. It's just another way that Jailbreak keeps the chaos going!

- DID YOU KNOW? -

Weapon skins were added for the first time to Jailbreak in a mega mini update in spring 2020!

91 ROBLOXIAN HIGH SCHOOL

Not all Town and City games are car-crazy, good versus bad chaos fests! Robloxian High school is much more relaxed and focuses on making friends, earning coins and accessorizing houses, avatars and vehicles. With hundreds of millions of visits and after nearly 4 million 'favorite' ticks, the development gang at Robloxian High School Group clearly knows how to create an epic adventure!

As a T&C game that crosses over heavily into role-playing, users explore the world of Robloxian, focusing on school, town and your own house. Check your schedule tab to see the lessons (periods) to attend, with the helpful navigate button giving you easy guidance to their location. You collect coins for attending classes – if only real school was this cool!

by Robloxian High School Group

QUICK STATS

👍 BEST GAMES **RATING: 86%**

VISITS: 800M+ CREATED: 30/6/2019 GENRE: Town & City

- DID YOU KNOW? -

Makers Robloxian High School Group like to add fresh updates and features, such as the love-heart themed House of Hearts for Valentines Day!

SO MUCH TO SEE!

Remember to use the green sprint button to speed you up and give you fast feet. If you're driving to school and are seriously late, just bash your vehicle straight into the building and you'll spring into school much quicker (and hopefully make it on time!).

Cars are a cool way to explore the Town and City landscape, with plenty of vehicle upgrades up for grabs if you have spare Robux. Gliders, though, are much more fun and if there's a skyscraper in the area, have a blast leaping from these structures for some serious freefalling!

Cooking class is a lesson that always licks the lips! Tucking into delish dishes like mac 'n' cheese or spaghetti gives you an appetite to get through the school day and, after filling your belly again at lunch, you can look forward to unlocking textbooks in brain-draining lessons such as science. RHS can be hard work at times!

When school's over, head home to start decorating and give your pad a party feel. Making a good home life is also an important part of this ROBLOX game. Remember that you don't need to be on foot all the time – the handy teleport tab, from the explore button, will magic you between zones in no time! Editing your avatar is a fun feature in Robloxian High school and the slick new Avatar Editor 3.0 allowed lots of new things, like changing the colour of accessories and retexturing items. Fancy, eh!

DRESSING UP

MUSIC

BLOXY WINNER!

5TH ANNUAL BLOXY AWARD

ROBLOXIAN HIGHSCHOOL

LET'S GO!

MEEPCITY

90

by **alexnewtron**

MeepCity is the most visited Roblox game in history! This social hangout and role-playing game has racked up more than 5 billion visits and 100,000 concurrent players. Impressive!

QUICK STATS

BEST GAMES **RATING: 91%**

VISITS: 5.1B+ CREATED: 23/2/2016 GENRE: Town & City

This was the first ROBLOX game to hit one billion visits, and in 2019 it reached well over four billion. This iconic game showcases action-packed adventure at its best! Avatars can play minigames, go fishing, build and furnish a house, attend parties, and interact with others on the server.

In MeepCity, there's no danger of being lonely as you can buy your own pet, called a Meep. Pop along to the Pet Shop to pick up a Meep for 100 coins. You can pick its colour and name it, too! Customization options range from new hairstyles or headgear for under 100 coins, to hats that cost thousands.

Smart "Meepers" don't waste cash on mega-pricey Meep items! Fishing is one of the main ways to generate coins. Bring along your charged up fishing rod and aim for the dark spots in the water where fish hide. Different fish can be sold to the Pet Shop for coins. Don't forget that you can only have 20 fish in your bucket!

Master Meepers are quick to upgrade their fishing rod by spending coins. After all, the better the rod, the more chance you will have of catching valuable and rare fish. Save up for the gold rod (1,500 coins) to up your chance of fishing out a prize catch!

WELCOME TO THE NEIGHBOURHOOD

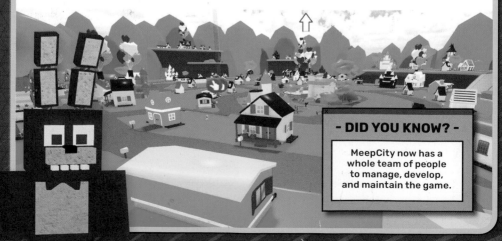

- DID YOU KNOW? -

MeepCity now has a whole team of people to manage, develop, and maintain the game.

WELCOME TO BLOXBURG

by **Coeptus**

89

Welcome to Bloxburg is quite an old game (by ROBLOX standards), but five years after its successful launch it still creates huge headlines! In 2019, this roleplay-heavy Town and City title joined the impressive list of games to stack up a billion visits, which was something only seven other games had achieved before. It also became the first paid access game to break the mark. Congrats to Coeptus!

Welcome to Bloxburg sells itself around the key words of 'relax, explore, work and build' – although not always in that order! With servers holding a maximum of 12 players, gameplay is busy enough without being overloaded and there's enough interaction for interesting adventures. Choose between a wide range of jobs at the beginning, such as cashier, ice cream seller, janitor and fisherman. Jobs pay a different amount of money and promotions to better-paid positions are achieved when tasks are done successfully. Make sure that you complete a shift to pick up that important paycheck!

Building is probably the most important part of Bloxburg for fans. So, simply click on the build mode icon to start constructing and designing! Really take pride in your plot and build the house of your dreams. And if you have any Robux, customize and decorate to make your creations stand out.

WHO LIVES IN THERE?

BLOXBURG CITY HALL

- DID YOU KNOW? -

In 2019, Welcome to Bloxburg recorded 100,000 concurrent players for the first time.

88

Pacifico 2:
PLAYGROUND TOWN

by **SynerG**

Away from the billion-plus visited titles of Mad and Meep City, smaller T&C genre games still pull in the players and offer hours of action through detailed adventures! Released at around the same time as Pacifico in 2017, Playground Town is one for true car fans with plenty of epic racing and upgrading exploits.

QUICK STATS

👍 BEST GAMES **RATING: 84%**

VISITS:	CREATED:	GENRE:
10M+	15/6/2017	Town & City

Make your team choice from either citizen, café worker, police officer, hospital worker, restaurant worker, office worker, racer and criminal. As a racer, for example, you're offered around 20 complimentary cars to pick from (other car series can be bought for Robux) and then it's time to set off around the town. Be a police officer and there are additional emergency vehicles at your fingertips!

Pacifico 2: Playground Town is a pretty relaxed game, with an easy pace and the chance to cruise the map at your own leisure. Snap up your own home or rest in the classy hotel, or there are quirky options like playing with your mobile phone, and grabbing essential food and energy drinks from the store.

The game doesn't offer leaderboards and points to collect, so if you're ultra competitive then it's going to disappoint. But dive straight in if you're a sandbox game fan and love driving around urban environments!

- DID YOU KNOW? -

Players take the driving very seriously, stopping at red lights and indicating all turns. They don't like damaging their beloved vehicles!

CHECK OUT MY NEW RIDE!

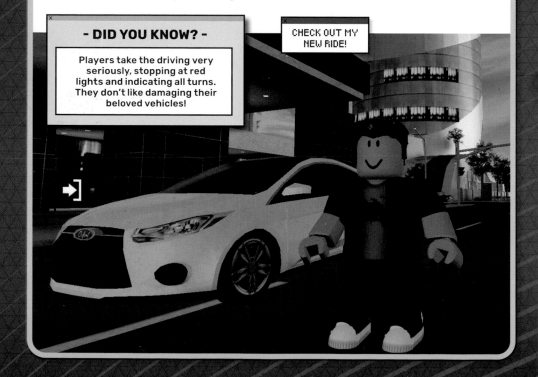

ROCITIZENS

by Firebrand1

Jobs, driving, socializing and customizing are some of the main missions for the folk of RoCitizens! The popular game has nearly 3 million favourites and tens of thousands on its servers at any one time, showing what a fashionable universe it is.

QUICK STATS	👍	BEST GAMES RATING: **85%**
	VISITS: 525M+	**CREATED:** 6/12/2013	**GENRE:** Town & City

Avatars can buy, build or import a home at the beginning of the game and blueprints (plans) can be picked for the type of property you want on your plot. All the daily info needed is handily displayed on your mobile phone – career progress, messages and even vehicle details are all there at the touch of a button. Daily cash bonuses are offered to keep gamers coming back, typically starting at $100 but ramping up to $3000 by day six!

Top developer Firebrand1 loves to release in-game codes for RoCitizens, which reward users with cash to use in the game, items and even glitzy trophies! When the game celebrated passing 500 million visits in early 2020, Firebrand1 released the code '500million' that dished out $5,000. Nice! Keep an eye on the ROBLOX homepage for details of these codes.

There's a massive choice of houses and furniture items to choose from so that you are able to deck your home out with, including new or themed pieces clearly displayed. The character editor and in-game emote buttons are fun to use, too. Just click the relax or sleep buttons to totally chill out in this Town and City playground! Enjoy.

- DID YOU KNOW? -

The game was originally called RoSims when it launched before being changed to RoCitizens in 2014.

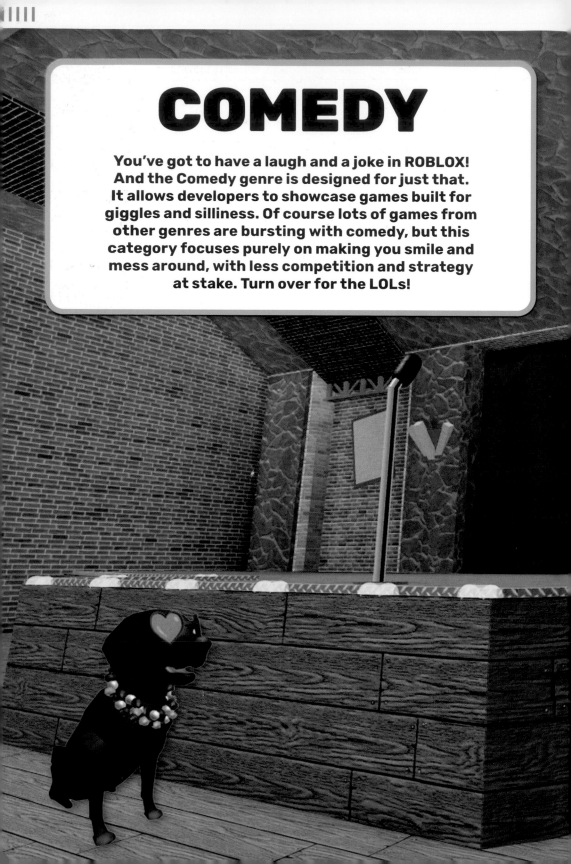

COMEDY

You've got to have a laugh and a joke in ROBLOX! And the Comedy genre is designed for just that. It allows developers to showcase games built for giggles and silliness. Of course lots of games from other genres are bursting with comedy, but this category focuses purely on making you smile and mess around, with less competition and strategy at stake. Turn over for the LOLs!

86

HOLE IN THE WALL

As you may expect, this comedy game involves a, uhm... hole in the wall! Using the idea from a 2008 British TV show, developer EricThePianoGuy hit upon a simple system. Basically, a big wall appears from behind a curtain, moves towards you and the only way to survive is by fitting through the holes in the wall as it passes you. Sounds easy, but it's not!

Join the game and you're placed in either the red or blue team. Games can be played solo or with other team members, but even in solo mode it's still the team's cause that you're playing for. The game automatically places you in the Play Area when it's your turn (there's no hiding from the wall!) and there's a message to tell you the

by EricThePianoGuy

QUICK STATS

👍 BEST GAMES **RATING:** **87%**

VISITS: | CREATED: | GENRE:
155M+ | 19/6/2009 | Comedy

difficulty of the wall that you'll face. Follow the on-screen instructions, such as to sit, lie down, dive or handstand, before quickly lining up and timing your move to fit through the hole as it reaches you. If you don't, you'll be splashed into the water behind!

Timing is crucial in this one – don't jump or dive too early – and work with your team so that you all fit through the gaps. While you wait your turn, watch how the

ARE YOU READY?

PLAY AREA

YOU CAN DO IT!

THAT'S A TOUGH ONE!

others deal with the wall and you may even be able to pick up some handy tips. A handstand, for example, makes you slim so that you can slide through even the tiniest gaps.

Don't go thinking that the gaps and holes stay the same size, and be prepared for crazy things like giant swinging bananas and spinning doughnuts that mess up your plans! The coins you collect for successful stages are displayed on the leaderboard as an incentive to get through the gaps.

Finally, try not to be put off by the funny pictures and characters that appear on the walls. It's bad enough having to jump through the difficult spaces without having a giant Minion, Adventure Time dude or Doctor Who racing towards you!

- DID YOU KNOW? -

Some of the walls are rated as 'impossible' to get through, although the gaps can actually be cleared. Just make sure you keep practicing!

COMEDY CLUB MEME UPDATE

by **Endless Amazement**

When games come along that are original and well made, ROBLOXIANS will flock to them. Despite Comedy Club Meme Update having no action-packed or fast-paced vehicles like some games, it's still an awesome area full of fun, LOLs and imagination! Over seven million visits in just a few months of release prove it's already a comedy classic.

If you fancy telling some jokes and gags, then step right up. Enter the comedy club and either get ready to take the stage and try to make the audience giggle, or hang around and decide if other users are funny or not. If you think the jokes you see are awful, throw tomatoes at the acts. There's even a tomato cannon to really tell joke tellers how awful they are!

It's all a bit of fun, so go to the side of the stage and get ready to type in your joke for the club. If people like it when it's revealed on stage, you'll earn smiles that can be used in the shop. Smiles are also picked up as daily rewards for going back to the game. Have a joke ready before you step up, or use the random jokes offered by the game. Good luck and have a good laugh!

QUICK STATS

👍 BEST GAMES **RATING: 90%**

VISITS: 7.5M+ **CREATED:** 1/12/2019 **GENRE:** Comedy

- DID YOU KNOW? -

You can use animations, laughs or cheering to react to the jokes being told in the comedy club.

I DON'T GET IT!

HAHAHAHA! HAHAHAHA!

84

THE COMEDY ELEVATOR

by **Client Sided Industries**

Any game that describes itself with the phrase 'warning: this game will make you laugh!' has a lot to deliver. Fortunately The Comedy Elevator does exactly that! The developer, Client Sided Industries, even added the warning that 'if you prefer philosophical games, I recommend you read a book!' So, don't just laugh off this advice!

QUICK STATS

👍 BEST GAMES **RATING: 85%**

VISITS: 8M+ | **CREATED:** 7/11/2019 | **GENRE:** Comedy

First off, this game is TOTALLY BONKERS. Sure, you can collect points and there are VIP areas to enter and passes and packages to buy, but really it's just a silly setup where you can pretty much run wild. From the lobby area, enter the elevator and see what ludicrous levels and areas it takes you to. When the doors open you could be faced with anything from obstacle courses to giant dogs or bouncing pigs – the minigames and adventures seem endless!

This is a great game to enjoy with friends. You can team up to take funny trips and tours via the elevator – just don't miss the amusing memes and posters on the walls as you go! Plus, if you're lucky enough, you could encounter the 'fart zone' and totally 'blow away' the other avatars around you! The Comedy Elevator is full of ups and downs (geddit?!) and you'll learn more each and every time the elevator doors open. Good luck!

TEE HEE!

HAHA! HERE WE GO!

- DID YOU KNOW? -

In early 2020, a game launched called The Natural Elevator... which is a mix of spooky and silly stuff!

MEDIEVAL AND FANTASY

You may have to search a little harder for Fantasy and Medieval games, but spot the right ones and you'll enter a world of action, myth and adventure unlike anywhere else in ROBLOXIA! Escape reality by venturing back in time to dangerous lands of battles and courage. Team up with dragons, monsters and ancient warriors in a world of endless opportunities. Enjoy!

WASTELAND DRAGON
ADVENTURES

83

Fantasy games can use a mix of game types, but they are always creative and adventurous, and encourage tactical thinking. Wasteland Dragon Adventures has picked up literally hundreds of thousands of fans in a very short time. As a fantasy-themed journey where dragons and evil mobs collide, it'll whisk your imagination away in an instant!

Teaming up and using your dragon to take on enemies, is one action needed in this game. But many players also love the nurturing option of the game. Dragons can be hatched and raised to become a powerful friend. From the dragon lair button, there's a choice of beasts to pick, and info such as the

by Sonar Studios

QUICK STATS

👍 BEST GAMES
RATING: 85%

VISITS: 55M+ CREATED: 15/7/2019 GENRE: Fantasy

- DID YOU KNOW? -

Developer Erythia's birthday is on 29 February – the leap year day! In 2020 she got to celebrate on the actual day and joked that she was only five!

SOAR THROUGH THE SKIES!

Tutorial
Point your camera and use W to fly!
To breathe fire, hold click! Let's defeat
some enemies with our fire!

creature's age, health, hunger and species is displayed. Keep an eye on the important HP (health) status too.

Dragons can also be bred to produce more mythical creations, and riding and flying high with them is all part of the Wasteland world. Facing up to floating islands and rulned toxic landscapes is to be expected, with higher levels reached through hard work and practise. Dragons have different flying speeds and demands, so choose your scary-looking companion wisely!

Don't worry if this all sounds a little complicated because there is a helpful tutorial option to take, which gets you familiar with the feel and features of Dragon Adventures.

Sonar Studios is the mega talented development group behind Wasteland Dragon Adventures. In around just six months, their fantasy creation racked up over 50 million visits. The group includes the ROBLOX developers TamBrush and Alertcoderf, with Erythia stepping in as the lead developer for the series. Erythla and her crew worked hard on the Wastelands update, which was unleashed in March 2020. It's no surprise that they hit their goal of 10,000 concurrent players in no time. Good work, dudes!

MEET MY NEW FRIEND

ONE STEP AT A TIME

82

KINGDOM LIFE II

by DevBuckette

The famous ROBLOX developer Boopbot first unleashed the hugely significant Kingdom Life series around 2009, with others, such as the DevBuckette and thelolguy301, stepping in later on. The sequence of games have collected the most 'favourite' ticks in the Medieval genre and fans have been eagerly awaiting KL III to drop into the game homepage by Boopbot some time soon!

QUICK STATS

BEST GAMES
RATING: 84%

VISITS:	CREATED:	GENRE:
48M+	3/7/2012	Medieval

In Kingdom Life II, players get a big boost of medieval fantasy goodness. Players can create their character and must make use of weapons and items to gain success on the map. Let your imagination drive you and once you're in the world of elves, ghosts, wolves and many more creatures, the fantasy will soon unravel.

There are some interesting Kingdom Life spin-off games to look out for on the games page. Kingdom Life II Classic by AyeItsJason, and Kingdom of Hreinngar also offer great fantasy role play action from a past world. Use your cunning powers and mythical knowhow to complete missions in a medieval map.

x
- DID YOU KNOW? -

You can choose a fun fantasy character name for your avatar and have this displayed above you during the game.

AHHHHH!

BEHOLD THE KINGDOM

MEDIEVAL WARFARE:
REFORGED

81

by Cody_Nelson

Select from the Greywolf, Korblox, Redcliff and Overseer kingdoms and join the ancient landscape. Take on other teams, collect weapons and mine resources to progress. Medieval Warfare: Reforged will keep you and your friends busy for hours.

Make clever use of the potions to boost your health as you set about one of the most important jobs of mining. Ores and trees need to be harvested and you can then trade these for coins. Coins are also given out through daily login rewards. The list of ores around the map is quite vast and precious products such as copper, gold, quartz, diamond, amethyst, zionite, cobalt and topaz can all be found from mines. Just take out your pickaxe and get to work!

Just watch out for enemy attacks in MK: R, though, because when you're busy trying to mine materials you're open to hostile approaches. There are various weapons available in the game and bigger and better weapons can be pocketed after successful mining. Remember that weapons can also be crafted at the blacksmiths.

Give your gameplay another advantage by getting gamepasses and special items. Ore and tree trackers will identify where they spawn and devices for speedier wood cutting, quick sprinting, efficient mining and damage bonuses all give you an epic edge in the kingdom.

WOULD YOU LIKE A BED FOR THE NIGHT?

- DID YOU KNOW? -

Every kingdom in the game has a king, which can be voted in. Do you fancy a royal reign?

INTO BATTLE!

ADVENTURE

Looking for adventure? Well, you've come to the right genre! These games can be pacey, unpredictable, testing, random and above all adventure-filled. From the multi million hits of Ninja Legends and Bee Swarm Simulator to smaller but hugely successful titles like Time Travel Adventures, let's take a look at what's needed for an awesome ROBLOX adventure.

NINJA LEGENDS

80

Scriptbloxian, the chief creator behind Scriptbloxian Studios, is the dude that millions of ROBLOX fans need to thank for the fun-packed Ninja Legends game! After creating the hugely popular Legends of Speed adventure title in early 2019, this fast-paced venture shot into ROBLOX in September 2019 and smashed nearly 700 million visits in just the first five months!

Ninja Legends deserves its spot as one of the hottest places for adventurous Robloxians to explore. The theme is to cruise and jump around a stack of cool islands, training your ninja to become the best and reaching for the leaderboards. Training is done by swinging epic weapons, like bamboo canes and swords, to collect Ninjitsu which can then be sold for coins and cashed in for superior weapons and damage making capabilities.

by **Scriptbloxian Studios**

QUICK STATS

👍 **BEST GAMES RATING: 92%**

VISITS: 800M+ **CREATED:** 22/9/2019 **GENRE:** Adventure

- DID YOU KNOW? -

Within just weeks of release, over 200,000 concurrent players were recorded playing Ninja Legends. Impressive!

MEOW!

MEOW!

CUTE PETS WILL HELP YOUR MARTIAL ARTS MISSIONS

Consistently rating over 90% by ROBLOX fans, Ninja Legends is classed in the same bracket as the popular Saber Simulator. Plus, with regular updates and code releases by Scriptbloxian it's kept fresh, fun and interesting. Got spare Robux to splash? Game Passes are the best value way to boost your ninja character – click the x 2 Ninjitsu, x 2 Coins and x 2 Speed buttons for a big gameplay increase!

Eliminating other ninjas will also increase your Chi levels when you swoop in for their 'souls'. Don't worry, it's nowhere near as scary as it may sound! The Chi currency is linked to purchasing pets and improving your training. You'll want to unlock training areas in your quest to become a lethal legend in this game.

Although companion Pets are an important part of Ninja Legends (giving you a multiplier increase), don't become too focused on them when you're a noob player getting to grips with it all. Become familiar with the islands first and the cute Pets will soon follow you and help your martial arts missions.

Don't forget to look up and reach for the skies in Ninja Legends too! The floating islands are reached easily by jumping and flipping in the air. Make the most of jump pads to launch you forcefully to higher ground. Jumping from atop trees gives you a sneaky lift and daily six-hour rewards offer a great Chi source!

Can you become the King of the Hill and enjoy meditating as the master of this ninja adventure? Join the server and start bossing it in fun battles to find out!

TRAIN WITH THE DOJO MASTER

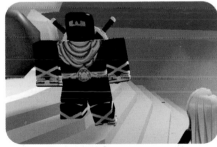

COLLECT CHI TO UNLOCK TRAINING AREAS AND PURCHASE NEW PETS

HIDE AND SEEK EXTREME

79

Hide and Seek Extreme is one of the most addictive games in the history of ROBLOX! It fits neatly in the Adventure genre because it's fast but not frantic, easy to understand and get involved with and can last for minutes or hours. So, why not open your eyes to the world of hide and seek?

The idea is very simple – at the start of a game, you and up to 10 others have to hide in a room or location and hope that the seeker doesn't find you. There are plenty of random places that will be chosen, ranging from bedroom and office to a kitchen and a backyard. Your task is to scurry off and take refuge – be quick because the seeker, called 'IT', unfreezes after one minute and will begin the search!

by **Tim7775**

BEST GAMES RATING: 89%

QUICK STATS

VISITS: 935M+

CREATED: 18/1/2015

GENRE: Adventure

There are dozens of places to hide, so players look for every little nook and cranny to disguise them. Try going high and low and use the square bounce pads to spring you into the air. The circular teleport pads will ping you between places in a flash, which is handy if you're hiding or seeking. Remember that the IT character can run faster than hiders, so there's little chance to escape!

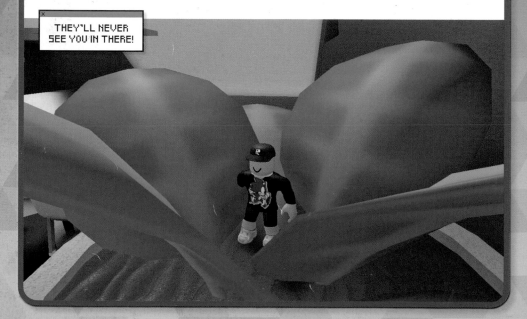

THEY'LL NEVER SEE YOU IN THERE!

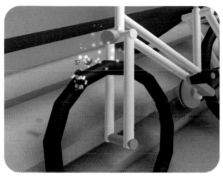

NOW IT'S MY TURN!

IT

As you hide, you have the option to spectate on the IT person to track their moves. The 'studs away' counter also shows you how near or far away they are and the seeker is surrounded by a glowing trail to make them stand out from the other players. Becoming the IT character is decided at the start of the game and seekers can use special powers to trap and detect the hiders, including glue drops, secret cameras and stun rays!

Try to collect coins around the locations and you'll get ten credits if you survive each four-minute chase. Coins can be used to purchase cool characters and items such as an IT multiplier, which boosts your chance of becoming the seeker.

So decide on your hiding tactic – will you stay put and hope you're not spotted, or move around in a game to evade detection? – and join the fun offered by this epic Adventure title. With thousands playing at any one time, Hide and Seek Extreme is the place to be seen... or not, ideally!

- DID YOU KNOW? -

While you wait to join a game or after you're eliminated, you can use the time to spy on other hiders and pick up hiding tips and techniques.

TIME TRAVEL ADVENTURES

78

The Adventure game genre opens all sorts of possibilities, including the chance for some exciting time travel! Time Travel Adventures soon grabbed the spotlight after landing on the games page in 2019 and Splitting Point Studios have done a great job of creating stylish gameplay with lots of possibilities.

Hunting down precious gems is the object of the game. Picking up important artifacts is also a priority as you venture through maps. The pressure is on to complete missions alongside other players and you'll often need to work as a team – for example, taking on gun-slinging Martians is no easy task if you're all alone!

by Splitting Point Studios

QUICK STATS

BEST GAMES **RATING: 83%**

VISITS: 35M+

CREATED: 29/5/2019

GENRE: Adventure

- DID YOU KNOW? -

Jandel is the lead scripter and owner in Splitting Point Studios, and is behind other cool games like Monster Simulator, FlameThrower Simulator and Floppy Fighters.

DISCOVER UNKNOWN TERRITORY

There are seven map areas to work through. They range from futuristic landscapes such as Mars, pre-historic places where T-rexes roam medieval and ancient Egyptian locations. A wise guide called Tim is your narrator and lead man to follow in most of these zones. So do pay attention to all of his directions and instructions. You have finite lives depending on the zone you're in, so think carefully about every move!

Time Travel Adventures is packed with many minigames, such as mazes and obstacle courses, which are good fun and can help you get closer to discovering the location of gems. Other missions are quite simple – for example, you need to find three sheep in the new Medieval Madness zone in the hope the helpful farmer can give you some clues to the gems. Un-baaah-lievable, hey?!

One great tip is to collect enough coins or Robux to pick up a Pet. These helpful animals have the power to attack your enemies and they can also increase coin multipliers. Time and patience are needed to master this Adventure game. Make sure you work hard and stick to a plan to collect the gems and artifacts and keep the baddies at bay.

MEET CRAZY CHARACTERS!

S EED U 4

by **Vurse**

Running and showing off your best parkour moves is the key to getting through the masses of levels and challenges in Speed Run 4. If you're not speedy and not on the run, then sadly you're doomed to failure in this game.

QUICK STATS

BEST GAMES
RATING: 82%

VISITS: 710M+

CREATED: 20/10/2014

GENRE: Adventure

Speed Run is a classic platform game, made famous in arcade titles like Mario and Sonic. Gamers are against the clock and as the levels progress in difficulty, the chance of collecting important rubies becomes even more of a challenge. There are around 30 unique levels to tackle and new dimensions are regularly added. Stars are also something to savour in Speed Run – the more of these collected, the more special modes can be opened.

Your avatar automatically flips in the air when you press the jump button and you'll need to work on your timing to leap between floating islands and pieces. Trails, dimensions, passes and sounds are the goodies up for grabs in the store once you have enough gems.

Levels need to be completed until you can move on, so give yourself enough time and practise to get the job done… or if you want to cheat a little, buy the 'skip level' option so that you don't have to complete them! Speed is vital, but remember that it's often a good idea to stop sometimes to have a look at the course ahead of you – just so that you don't make a silly move and are taken back to the start.

- DID YOU KNOW? -

Vurse is a big fan of space travel and interplanetary missions, which is why Speed Run has a massive galactic feel to it.

HOW FAST CAN YOU GO!?

SHARKBITE

by **Abracadabra**

With anywhere between 10,000 to 20,000 concurrent players, the waters can be busy (and frightening!) around SharkBite. The choice is to be a survivor or the shark, and to destroy each other on the seas – although the probability of getting the shark role is low each time! Survivors can equip themselves with armour and protection to take on this fish-based fight!

QUICK STATS

👍 BEST GAMES **RATING: 87%**

VISITS: 470M+ **CREATED:** 10/4/2017 **GENRE:** Adventure

The key is to collect rewards known as shark teeth. These are handed out each time you complete a time-based mission in the water and the goal is to save up for a top-level boat such as the SWAT boat or deluxe yacht. In mega machines like those, your safety is massively boosted! Handy, eh?

While you're out on the water in smaller vessels, take care not to capsize your equipment as you'll be exposed and open to attack. Be careful not to use up all of your ammo too quickly and if you are having to shelter on top of an upturned boat, sometimes hiding just above the water is a better way to stay out of the scary shark's vision!

The shark's green health bar is displayed at the top of the screen. Watch this for how well the shark is fairing in the challenge. Once the screen displays the scary message of 'the shark has been released', it's time to scan the sea for any sight of that dark fin moving in on you!

ARGHHH!

AHOY THERE!

BEE SWARM SIMULATOR

by Onett

There's always been a great big 'buzz' around this game! Since launching in 2018 it has rocketed towards the magic 1 billion visits mark. Onett is such a red-hot developer that the title was named Game of the Year at the 2019 Bloxys!

QUICK STATS

👍 **BEST GAMES RATING: 91%**

VISITS: 810M+
CREATED: 21/3/2018
GENRE: Adventure

Bee Swarm Sim has stayed around the front page of ROBLOX for such a long time because it's simple, pretty looking and addictive to play. The aim is to collect pollen from flowers and make some tasty honey, all with the help of your friendly swarming bees! Bees hatch from honeycombs and you'll begin to see the pollen count rise on your backpack. In the shop, the honey you make lets you purchase super helpful tools like a bigger backpack and a faster scooper.

Watch out for the nasty bugs and monsters that can try to kill you! But don't worry, because your super swarm will protect you from attacks. Bees have different strengths and abilities, so keep a watch for the tokens they spawn. Keep close to the bears that wander around as they deliver helpful quests. If a bear has something to say, it has a yellow exclamation mark displayed in front of it. Good luck and bee-have yourself!

WHAT A BUSY BEE!

BUZZ BUZZ

- DID YOU KNOW? -

Developer Onett says that the biggest influence he's had in making the game was the Snow Shoveling Simulator game. He absolutely loves that!

DON'T PRESS THE BUTTON 2

by On-Point Productions

There are several games like this on the ROBLOX home page, with the original Don't Press the Button appearing in spring 2019 and a few 'Don't Touch...' spinoffs sprinkled around the website. DPTB 2 has proven very popular, scoring 40 million visits in just a few months of it dropping.

QUICK STATS

BEST GAMES **RATING: 83%**

VISITS: 40 M+

CREATED: 28/1/2020

GENRE: Adventure

This game could be placed in the minigame genre as there are lots of activities and games to explore in a limited amount of time. The action is completely random and each time the button is pressed, a new mission appears. These can be as simple as running between coloured squares, jumping on floating islands using giant gum or dodging falling rockets. Completing a speed run across a floating obstacle course is much trickier, but if you do reach the end

you'll get to wear a cool crown as the king or queen of the game!

Natural disasters are a hazard to conquer in Don't Press the Button 2. One of the scariest of all is an earthquake – staying on the island during this rumble sure requires a lot of effort! Try to collect coins on the map and use these to get game passes and boosts. The grapple hook item is awesome as it can fling you to wherever you want!

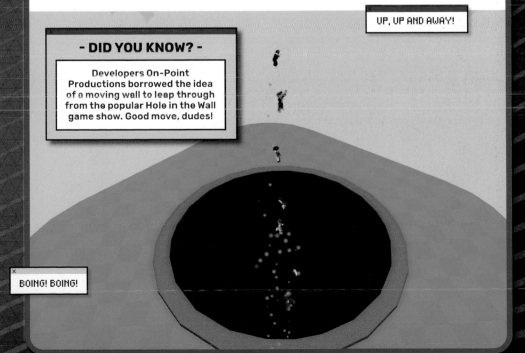

UP, UP AND AWAY!

- DID YOU KNOW? -

Developers On-Point Productions borrowed the idea of a moving wall to leap through from the popular Hole in the Wall game show. Good move, dudes!

BOING! BOING!

PHANTOM FORCES

by **StyLiS Studios**

Packed with detailed weapons and lots of customization and upgrade options, it's easy to see why FPS lovers rank Phantom Forces as one of the genre's premier places for an exciting shootout! There are two teams involved, with the Ghosts taking on the Phantoms and much at stake around the various maps.

QUICK STATS

👍 BEST GAMES **RATING: 84%**

VISITS: 840M+ **CREATED:** 31/8/2015 **GENRE:** FPS

New players should ignore the stat-heavy weapon lists and selections at first. It can be more of a distraction as you begin getting used to the tactics of the game. When you're clued up on that, though, feel free to dive into the details of primary and secondary weapons, grenades, items and all the rest to become an expert!

From the lobby, your vital stats are clearly displayed between games. These include your rank, XP, Kills, Deaths and Kill Death Ratio (KDR). There's a big incentive to boost these, and seeing the next weapon you can unlock as a reward should have you

sharpening your sights around the maps. Players have the chance to vote for a map in the next game, including areas like Mirage, Rig, Mall, Warehouse and Highway Lot, and game modes such as Capture the Flag and Team Deathmatch.

In Capture the Flag, teams must retrieve and return each other's flags, or pick up the most flags during game time. With the credits won, the customizations can begin and there are opportunities for case openings to boost your weaponry.

SET A TRAP AND WAIT FOR VICTORY!

- DID YOU KNOW? -

Update 15 in 2019 added cool new features like the new third person muzzle flash effects and improved enemy radar positioning mechanics.

72

BIG PAINTBALL

by **BIG Games**

For some games, their title describes exactly what they are, and this is one big paintball party! Demonstrating that first person shooters are not all hardcore battles, BIG Paintball delivers a crazy and colourful splash of fun and laughs.

QUICK STATS

👍 BEST GAMES **RATING:** **82%**

VISITS: 181M+ CREATED: 27/7/2019 GENRE: FPS

Just like the sport of paintball in real life, the aim is to splat pellets of paint against the opposition. This is called tagging and is the key element in this fun game, which quickly picked up over 180 million visits in just over six months from release. Games are team based or in the chaotic free-for-all mode against the clock, with credits collected for the tagging levels achieved. Superior weapons can be unlocked depending on the progress you make and for missions such as kill streaks.

Players want to quickly upgrade their paintball weapon from the one-click capability of the default semi-automatic at spawn, with Uzis, M4s and SMGs – all offering much better power on the map. Tags also reward

you with new abilities, including radar, sentry and drone skills. These focus on identifying opponents more easily and allowing you to be efficient with your movements. If you can strike other gamers without them even knowing your were on their trail, then your success rate will sky rocket!

Keep an eye out for limited time items, many of which are free, especially around holiday times and key events like Halloween and Easter. The free Super Dope Gun from February 2020 was snapped up by most players in the blink of an eye!

x

- DID YOU KNOW? -

The dev studio behind BIG Paintball released four cool game updates within just a couple of months of the game's release to keep things feeling fresh!

MAKE A SPLASH!

71

ARSE AL

by ROLVe Community

First person shooter games don't come much bigger or more exciting than Arsenal! Bursting onto the scene in 2015 and after a big update a few years later, fans of this genre keep coming back for the weapon-based adventures. It's common to have tens of thousands of concurrent players on the Arsenal servers.

QUICK STATS

BEST GAMES
RATING: 92%

VISITS: | CREATED: | GENRE:
670M+ | 18/8/2015 | FPS

After toggling through the choice of skin colours at the beginning of the game, players then deploy and choose a coloured team to be part of. There's a range of maps to play on, from fairgrounds and urban scenes to community-made zones, and teams battle together in order to eliminate other groups. Being able to run while firing is vital and it could take a while to get used to the fast pace of Arsenal.

Weapons begin at a standard level, but after eliminations you'll usually get an upgrade that makes you more of a menace on the battleground. Once you see others with a big machine gun, for example, you'll defo want one too!

The kill count is important and you'll want to boost your rank in the game. If you're taken out by an opponent, you run the risk of your weapon being downgraded and your power taking a serious zap.

Try spectating on a game if you're new to Arsenal. It will help you pick up the rules and some handy fighting tips, too. You can also change camera angles and the players you follow. In Arsenal, game modes such as 'randomizer' can become a bit of a free for all as random weapons spawn. You'll be watching the game clock count down and hoping you make it to the end! There are one-on-one modes as well as team tussles, so try not to run out of ammo just at the time you need to make a crucial strike, as there won't be team-mates to help you!

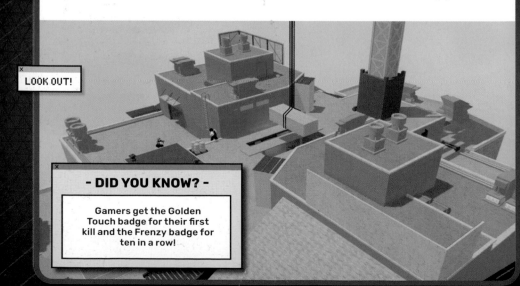

x
LOOK OUT!

x
- DID YOU KNOW? -

Gamers get the Golden Touch badge for their first kill and the Frenzy badge for ten in a row!

70 COUNTER BLOX

by ROLVe Community

Here's another smash hit FPS game from the ROLVe Community – the clever bods behind the awesome Arsenal! There's a lot of technical detail in Counter Blox and it's a close replica of the popular CS:GO video game. Expect a top shootout and enough action to keep you aiming down your sights for hours!

QUICK STATS		
👍	BEST GAMES RATING:	**82%**
VISITS: 181M+	CREATED: 27/7/2019	GENRE: FPS

Counter Blox is a dramatic team FPS, with five v five matchups across a variety of worldwide maps. It's counter terrorists (CTs) against terrorists and the CTs' mission is to eliminate the bad guys and diffuse the battle before they do some serious damage. Against the clock, players take to the maps, making the most of the weapons they have at their disposal.

Dropped items can be picked up around the map and the detail given about the weapons is very impressive – damage, fire rate, accuracy and recoil control stats are all displayed – plus there are extras like cool Kevlar armour jackets. From the skins section of the store, cases can be opened with your credits earned and gear can be collected at either standard, uncommon, rare, elite or legendary status. Remember that your items can be traded with other players if you like and not necessarily just equipped by you.

The graphics, engine and sound quality for Counter Blox are some of the best in the FPS slot, allowing for fast and smooth games. Most top-level players prefer the method of tap firing against the opposition, which means you fire slower single shots rather than keeping the trigger down for auto fire. This reduces spray and increases accuracy, especially at distance.

- DID YOU KNOW? -

Your team is tracked at the top of the screen in each game – a skull and crossbones symbol signifies a player who has been taken out!

HORROR
AND SCI-FI

These two genres go hand in hand – science fiction
can be often be horrifying and horror games lean
heavily into sci-fi worlds! Mixing scary scenes with
monsters, weapons, intergalactic spacecraft and
science-based missions is all part of the plan
in these two genres. Look over some of the best
of the bunch...

FLEE THE FACILITY

Flee the Facility is awesome – games don't rack up over one billion visits unless they are totally kicking it! Although officially classed in the Horror genre, it slots neatly into Adventure too and actually isn't that scary. Well, maybe just a little bit!

by A.W. Apps

QUICK STATS

BEST GAMES **RATING: 90%**

VISITS: 1.4B+

CREATED: 1/7/2017

GENRE: Horror

Set up for five players, Flee the Facility's simple idea is that you team up with up to three others to be classed as 'survivors'. You must explore a map in order to hack between three to five computers, depending on the number of players, and then try to escape through one of two exits. The only problem is... the Beast!

In Flee the Facility, one player is assigned as the Beast character. Their mission is to capture the survivors and drag them to freezing pods where their health is drained before they are eventually eliminated. If the Beast eliminates all players, he or she is the victor. It's whacky, fun and needs excellent teamwork!

BASH! SMASH!

DROP AND SMASH!

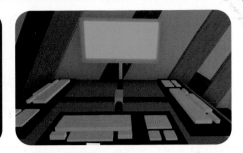

The Beast captures survivors by knocking them down and taking them to the nearest pod. The other players can race in and release a teammate from a pod, so keep an eye on the red health bars at the top of the screen to see who is suffering in your game. Obviously you're at risk by doing this as the Beast may be lurking, or 'camping' as it's known in the game, and could rush in and knock you down too.

As a survivor in Flee the Facility, you'll often find yourself crawling through vents and holes in walls to escape. The Beast can also do this if it de-equips its weapon. Survivors can also hide in lockers and under tables, but don't forget that as a standing target you will be easier to strike.

The key element is to hack computers quickly. If three survivors hack one at the same time, the process is sped up. If you force an error as you hack, you will give away your location and the Beast will have the advantage. Be quick and be clever.

As the Beast gets nearer you'll hear a distant breathing sound and a distinct soundtrack will play – use these as your cue to make an escape or hide. It's also a good idea to keep a clear view of doors and windows while you hack so that the Beast can't creep up and make a surprise entrance. Finally, don't make the mistake of becoming an AFK, meaning a player who is 'away from keyboard', as the Beast will easily pick you off. Your teammates won't like it either as you won't be helping the mission!

68 MURDER MYSTERY 2

Being the Xbox Game of the Year at the 2020 Bloxys is proof that Murder Mystery 2 is up there with the very best ROBLOX games of all time! And if you need further evidence, the 2 billion-plus visits and nearly 8 million favourite ticks show that the community cares deeply about this title – the figures are nearly as scary as the action involved!

Each MM2 server sees a maximum of 12 users in action, split between 1 murderer, 1 sheriff and up to ten players, known as the innocents. The sheriff and the murderer are selected randomly from the players and there's quite a small chance that you'll be selected as either. The game maps change regularly but once you spawn in a location, get ready for a frenzied

by Nikilis

QUICK STATS

👍 BEST GAMES RATING: **91%**

VISITS: 2.4B+   CREATED: 18/1/2014   GENRE: Horror

x
- DID YOU KNOW? -
In chat, if a player types 'gg' this means they're saying that was a 'good game'!

x
YOU CAN SEE IT ALL FROM UP HERE!

x
- DID YOU KNOW? -
Innocents will spawn with a weapon but they aren't able to use it.

chase as the evil player tries to hunt down the innocents before the sheriff can stop them in their tracks. It's tense, and a little terrifying!

The sheriff spawns with a useable weapon and is the only player able to defeat the murderer. The innocents work closely with the sheriff, though, and if they witness any eliminations and work out who the murderer is, the information will be quickly passed to the sheriff. A good tip for the murderer is to act as stealthy and as ordinary as possible, just so that no one suspects you. The game is a race against the clock and the appointed murderer aims to wipe out the players, including the sheriff, for an overall victory.

Players pick up coins around the map, which can be used in the shop for cool items such as weapons, effects and powers, and XP is also awarded. This XP is given out if the murderer takes down the players but also dished out if players survive each game. Innocents should be alert to a weapon being dropped by a sheriff, as this means it can be picked up and the chance to become a hero and gain extra XP arises.

When you are eliminated early, use the spectate function to spy on and pick up tips from other players. If you have chat enabled, this is an important tool – getting messages between innocents improves your chances of solving the murder mysteries!

67 GALAXY

Sci-Fi and Horror genre games often go hand in hand, mixing fearsome gameplay with a futuristic and fantasy-based theme. For science fiction fans, there's plenty to choose from in the ROBLOX Games page and the long-standing Galaxy adventure always pulls in a lot of followers.

To begin your Galaxy quest, you'll need to join a faction from a user-prepared list which changes frequently. Mining and space crafts form the main part of your operation. There's plenty of mining and cargo ships on screen and involved with your gameplay. Users take ships from terminals and aim to

by rcouret

QUICK STATS

BEST GAMES
RATING: **89%**

VISITS: CREATED: GENRE:
14.1M+   3/1/2015   Sci-Fi

mine for ores. Loading up your ship's ore hold is essential for the galactic economy. After using the cool ore laser function, you must dock and dump the gathered materials in return for building supplies that can be used to craft ships.

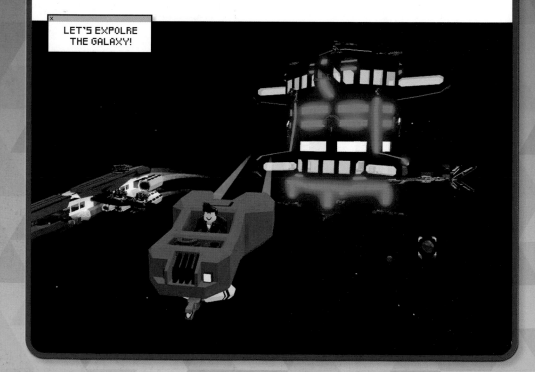

LET'S EXPOLRE THE GALAXY!

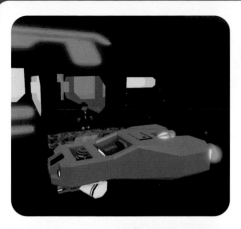

WHOOSH!

WHERE NEXT?

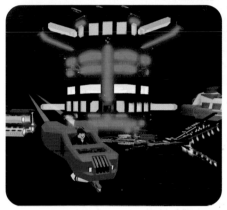

Mining can be dangerous in the world of Galaxy where combat ships can have guns, turrets or both. It's best to fight back at raids in groups if you can and remember that faster, smaller ships are harder to track and hit, too. Lasers have good effects against any shields and the warp function could help you relocate and take time to safely repair any damage from conflict.

The workings of star bases, warehouses, loyalty bonuses, materials, credits, codes and loads more will take time to get used to, but for true sci-fi people these technical details will be explored and understood. New players should always read through the helpful tutorial given at the start!

Los Angeles-based developer rcouret has a long history in producing really successful games for ROBLOX. If you're a sci-fi fanatic and like Galaxy, then check out one of his other games called Galaxy Arcade. The developer describes it as a little easier to play than the original Galaxy. With over four million visits and plenty of inter-galactic action, it's worth a visit. Field of Battle is another of his titles and although it's not sci-fi, check it out for medieval fighting chaos!

INNOVATION ARCTIC BASE

66

by Innovation Inc.

Two sci-fi ROBLOX fans are responsible for the fun and games over at Innovation Arctic Base. If you like experiments and crunching facts and figures in the brainy world of science, then say a big thanks to developers Rolijok and madattak from Innovation Inc. for their hard work!

QUICK STATS

BEST GAMES **RATING: 85%**

VISITS:	CREATED:	GENRE:
21M+	8/9/2017	Sci-Fi

For science lovers, choosing to be on the Scientists' team will likely take preference over joining the Security force. Scientists must undertake experiments deep under the Arctic surface, and only these mega clever characters can operate the hi-tech machinery dotted around. Scientists have exclusive access to the science-only rooms. A scientist's aim is to find and claim a plot (room) so that they can begin to build their own in-game laboratory. Setting up the lab is a bit like normal building games and the easy Build Mode option allows players to select and place important testing and office equipment.

Away from the special labs, other areas can only be entered if you're on the Security team – the scanners

by the doors will simply deny you access! Being in this team gives you cool weapons and you can even access the security cameras to check for unwanted intruders to the underground areas. Beware that your arsenal only has a certain clip size and will need time to reload as you continue shooting.

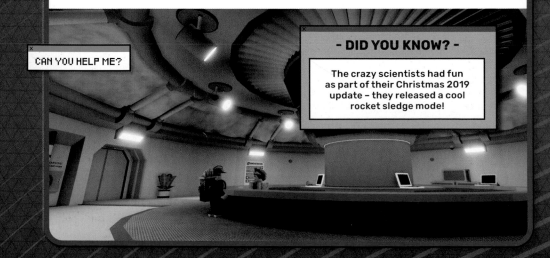

CAN YOU HELP ME?

- DID YOU KNOW? -

The crazy scientists had fun as part of their Christmas 2019 update – they released a cool rocket sledge mode!

INNOVATION LABS

by **madattak**

The clever developer madattak certainly loves science-based fun, with the Innovation Labs game coming before Arctic Base. It's still attracting visitors today, just as it was a decade ago, so give it a try and you won't be let down.

QUICK STATS

BEST GAMES **RATING:** **80%**

VISITS: 28.4 M+ | CREATED: 18/3/2010 | GENRE: Sci-Fi

The idea is to visit the secret underground research lab and, as a scientist, conduct tests and experiments while all the time being watchful of the central nuclear reactor core. There are different sections to explore away from the lobby, including the zero gravity room, hover car room and portal room. Some areas are covered as classified zones, such as Sector D, which has a cloning machine.

The numbers around the reactor need to be monitored closely, as the most dangerous thing that can happen is it reaching 2000°C and sparking a big meltdown. This begins a corruption and the threat of the labs self destructing! At 900°C a warning alarm begins, repeating if it rises to 1300°C before a major sound-off at 1650°C. There are ways to evade the meltdown, including running early on, reaching escape vents

- DID YOU KNOW? -

To use the Insta-Travel tool in the lobby you need to be a member of the Innovation Inc. group!

or portals and hiding in the shower areas. These won't always work, but your best chance of survival is to be quick and react sharply to the reactor rising!

The Innovation Shop has plenty of epic items and if you're lucky enough to collect stuff like the Anti-Zombie Taser, Jetpack, Flashlight or Speed Coil, then you'll greatly improve your chances of carrying out important research and surviving the volatile lab areas.

LET'S GO THIS WAY!

64 PIGGY CHAPTER 7

by MiniToon

MiniToon must be mad-keen on pigs, because this Piggy game and the following 'Piggy But It's 100 Players' spin-off are both packed with trotter chaos! In just a few months it rocketed to the 500 million mark and new chapters keep being released due to its amazing popularity. Chapter 7, in March 2020, was known as the Metro update and the giant Piggy character had a Zompiggy skin!

So, why's this cute piggy-based game in the horror category? Well, the Piggy here isn't super cute and is more interested in eliminating the other players, or at the very least capturing and stopping them escaping! Piggy coins, called tokens, must be collected around the maps by escaping when you're the survivor.

QUICK STATS

👍 BEST GAMES **RATING: 90%**

VISITS: 465M+ **CREATED:** 23/1/2020 **GENRE:** Horror

The person controlling Piggy is decided at the start, so it could be you, another player or a bot (NPC) in control. The Piggy's job is to simply capture and touch all of the survivors. Players must pick up certain items like tools and keys to help them to escape.

It's a good idea to quickly become familiar with the layout of rooms and areas you're in to avoid being trapped by the Piggy. You may find, however, that some of the handy tunnels or hatches for disappearing through are too big for the Piggy. Sometimes just hiding behind a door can be enough to fool Piggy off your scary scent!

- DID YOU KNOW? -

For the first few months, the game stayed in the testing mode, called 'alpha', but it still attracted hundreds of millions of users!

THIS LITTLE PIGGY DOES NOT GO TO MARKET

ZOMBIE ATTACK

by **Horror Portals**

Do you think zombies aren't real? You may think again after a few goes of this frighteningly fun zombie fighting game! It's packed with monster madness but if you practise and get your shooting targets sorted, you'll soon be slaying your way to success! What are you waiting for?

QUICK STATS

👍 BEST GAMES **RATING: 83%**

VISITS:	CREATED:	GENRE:
670 M+	12/12/2017	Horror

At the start of the game, newbies are directed towards the basic entry level gameplay. Playing at a higher level requires more experience as top levels need to be unlocked, which is a good idea as you get used to the tactics of defeating the enemies. It's a simple shoot 'em up game – zombies attack in waves and you and the team must fend them off with your weapons. The more you take down, the more cash and XP you gain, which means you can trade basic weapons for mega machines like a shotgun and uzi. Grenades can be very effective from a distance!

Watch out for the Boss zombie – you'll know who it is because it is three times as large as the other creepy creatures! Your melee weapon does let you deal damage close up, but it's best to fire at a distance with automatic weapons. Plus, getting to a high spot increases your vision and range.

Zombies can attack from any angle or direction, so keep scanning the horizon for approaching fearsome foes. All sorts of upgrades can be collected from the shop, so use cash or spare Robux to get ready to repel the waves!

ROLE-PLAYING GAMES

Take on the role of a cool ROBLOX character and join an adventurous journey, often facing enemies and having to collect cash in some of the biggest role-playing games in ROBLOX! RPGs can also be quite calm and cute – think Adopt Me and Horse World. Check out these, plus plenty more awesome role-playing titles that millions of users enjoy!

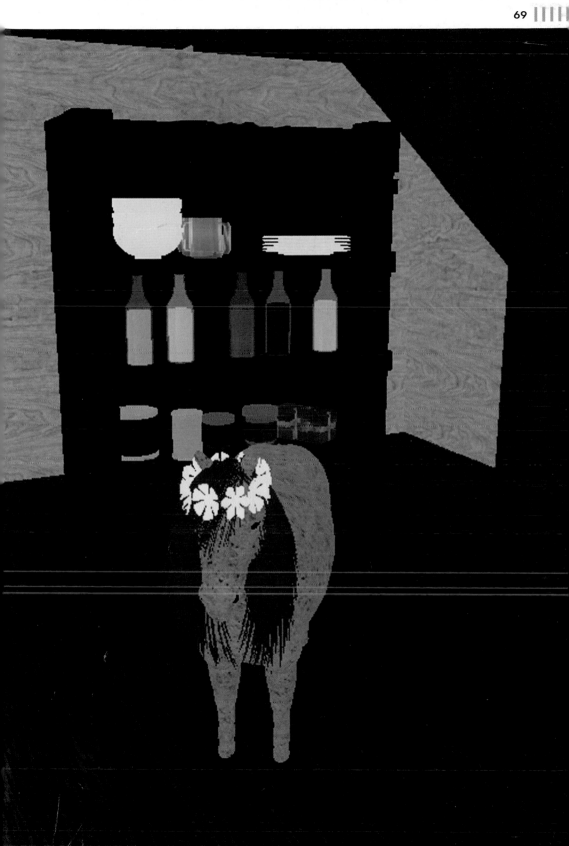

62 ADOPT ME

Have you ever seen the ROBLOX front page without Adopt Me featured? It's very unlikely given that hundreds of thousands of ROBLOXIANS play it at the same time. In fact, it holds the record for concurrent players – set at 517,000 in October 2019 – and is the second most visited game of all time behind MeepCity. Wow!

The brainchild of technical director NewFissy and creative director Bethink, Adopt Me is a sophisticated and seemingly endless role-playing world where players choose to either be a parent or a baby. You need to approach players and ask to add them to your family, then you can adopt a little 'un. Alternatively, you can be the

by DreamCraft

QUICK STATS

👍 BEST GAMES RATING: **92%**

VISITS: 5B+
CREATED: 14/7/2017
GENRE: RPG

- **DID YOU KNOW?** -

Adopt Me has won loads of awards and picked up the Bloxy for Studio of the Year in 2020.

IT'S A BRIGHT NEW DAY!

one that's adopted and cared for. In a family, there are four important needs of a baby that must be monitored and looked after – these are hunger, fun, cleanliness and sleepiness. Each of these needs is represented by a status bar, which will reduce if the needs are not looked after appropriately.

When needs are cared for well, parents receive a bigger daily paycheck each time. These awards provide Bucks, the in-game currency, which can then be used in the shop for cool stuff like pets, teleport powers and the ability to sell food and drink to earn more Bucks. Pets became a big part of the Adopt Me universe in 2019, with players then able to adopt cute creatures like cats, dogs and unicorns. Pets also have lots of demands and needs, although these are different to a baby's. Pets can come with you to school and ride alongside you if you have a car!

Adopt Me also takes great pride in a gamer's ability to customize their homes and create a unique space that's personal to them. Players spawn in their homes and along with creating a fresh look for your avatar, there's a whole world of designing and dressing to your taste to explore!

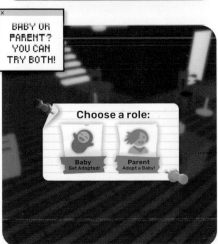

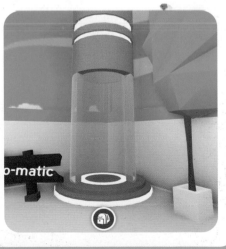

61 SUPER HERO LIFE II

RPGs are all about putting yourself in another character's shoes, so now it's time to slip on some superhero size nine boots and get ready for battle! Fuelled by the craze for Marvel and DC crime-fighting movies and video games, this ROBLOX masterpiece continues to attract new visitors desperate for a slice of supernatural chaos.

Developer CJ_0yer already had the success of the original SHL game to build on. Along with the rest of the Nightcycle Studios team they set about making SHL2 with bigger maps, more buildings and many more suit varieties compared to the first. The game has two mode options, called combat or roleplay mode. Choose roleplay as a new player and you'll have

by CJ_0yer

QUICK STATS

BEST GAMES RATING: 88%

VISITS: 580M+
CREATED: 24/9/2016
GENRE: RPG

the chance to get to grips with the map, moving around and, most importantly, flying! It can be tricky at first and you'll need to watch your health and energy bars as you zoom through the sky. This mode has no fighting and is designed so that you can experience your powers and craft your own suit.

Making superhero suits is totally epic! Get the look just right for you, editing colours and garments for a fashion style

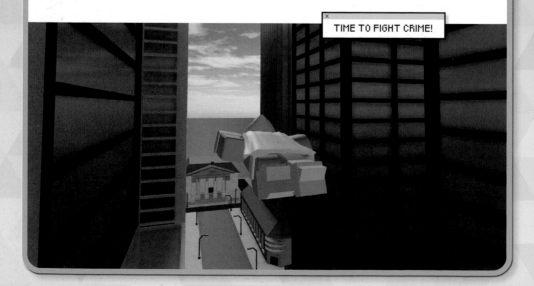

TIME TO FIGHT CRIME!

YOU MUST PROECT
THE CITY!

that means business. Chest armor, body armor, masks, hoods, boots, capes and stacks more can be added and crafted. In full combat mode, you can take on quests to chase down villains and earn gems and super credits to use in the shop. This game mode is full of action, so be on your guard and ready to deploy your powers!

Heroes to choose from include the awesome Red Rage, Light Void, The Enforcer, Storm Lord and Snow Sister. Each has a distinct look and vibe and their powers range from martial arts to blizzard spins and punches, with weapons including lasers, rifles and pistols. Mysterious strengths like force field, invisibility and camouflage have all appeared in SHL2, so be ready for some cool game twists at any moment!

- DID YOU KNOW? -

There's also a Super Hero Life III game to try, once you conquer this experience!

60 SURVIVOR

by **Peak Precision Studios**

QUICK STATS

👍 **BEST GAMES RATING: 84%**

VISITS:	CREATED:	GENRE:
205M+	6/11/2016	RPG

"Do you have what it takes to beat the odds and become the Sole Survivor?" asks the game's official ROBLOX description. Survivor is all about thinking quickly and smartly to prolong your stay on an island after leaving a ship. It gives the RPG genre a quite unusual, but fun and provoking, game.

You take on the role of a survivor from a ship. After all the players vote for either the Redemption or Classic game mode, players then decide on who the two tribe leaders are and the two teams are picked. As you've probably guessed, there's lots of voting and things to decide on in Survivor! The in-game guide is called Jeff and he will advise you on the team and individual challenges to take. The losers have to face the Tribal Council, where one player will be voted out. Winning immunity by performing well in the challenges is absolutely vital!

The challenges can involve skill and dexterity. Eventually the game will arrive at the point where the tribes merge and it becomes every player battling for their own survival! The winner of these mini games earns the right not to be voted off the island at the Tribal Council votes. Random spawn advantages appear around the island, offering things like a vote steal, a vote block, hints and extra votes. These can be very helpful in keeping your place among the rest of the crew. Try hitting the spectate button if you're unsure of the main rules so that you can observe how the more experienced survivors go about their business.

SMOOTH SAILING...

... BUT NOT FOR LONG!

59 HORSE WORLD

by Virtuality World

You can find most of your favourite things in ROBLOX, and for horse riders, owners and fans, the Horse World game takes you away to a land where ponies, foals, horses (and unicorns!) roam free. It mixes role-playing with fantasy, as well as a strong hint of collection as you pick up different breeds and customizations.

QUICK STATS

👍 BEST GAMES **RATING: 83%**

VISITS:	CREATED:	GENRE:
147M+	18/11/2017	RPG

When you spawn in, a player must pick between a range of worlds recommended for either tablet, PC or mobile platforms. They are all lush open settings with idyllic locations where these fabulous creatures can explore and be content. There are around 40 types of horses to choose from, including small Shetland ponies and foals, to prized Arabians and Friesians. Some of the more fancy breeds require you to have a game pass or to join a ROBLOX user group.

Take your time to edit and create your own horse at the beginning. This involves picking the tall, body, hooves, mouth and chin colours plus lots more options. Collect money and rewards to earn items and accessories as you venture, with the options to collect carts and enter barns as well. There's a lot of imagination involved in Horse World and the pace is gentle, which can be a welcome break in ROBLOX if you're used to playing more dramatic and fast-paced games.

WHICH HORSE WILL YOU CHOOSE?

- DID YOU KNOW? -

Instead of playing as a horse, you can choose to spawn as a human – but that kinda goes against the point of playing Horse World!

NEIGH!

58

LIMITLESS RPG

by **Core Productions 2.0**

Core Productions, lead by the designer Breezy, slowly but surely picked up a cult following after dropping Limitless RPG into the genre right at the end of 2019. Within a couple of months it clicked past the 500,000 visits level and the studio gave away a free XP potion to players. What a way to celebrate!

QUICK STATS

👍 BEST GAMES **RATING: 82%**

VISITS:	CREATED:	GENRE:
1M+	31/12/2019	RPG

Based in an ancient world with castles and warriors galore, the makers call it the "land of killed or be killed." Scary! The setup is that your castle has lost its finest crusaders in the Limitless War, and now you must protect the fortress from future enemy raids. Training, exploring and scouring the medieval map for enemies are your primary objectives. This hard work rewards you with precious gold coins. Use this currency to purchase new weapons from the store. Gold will also be able to upgrade the arsenal you already have.

Weapons have rarities and you'll soon want to be equipped with a better tool than the common default melee sword.

Take down the crowds of warriors that wander around and see your XP and gold levels shoot up!

Work out an effective way to run and slay your enemies, keeping an eye on your progress on the leaderboards. There are more than 150 weapons to cycle through and with 13 exciting zones, Limitless RPG will seem like a, uhm... limitless RPG game!

MEET THE VILLAGERS

57

FreeZe TAg

by **Connor VIII**

Freeze Tag has been around for a few years, but recently its popularity began to go up and up. It finally smashed the 100 million visits mark and there were even official ROBLOX Freeze Tag toys released in the summer of 2019! This adventurous RPG places you in the position of running away or tagging for victory – it's quick and chaotic!

QUICK STATS

👍 BEST GAMES **RATING: 87%**

VISITS:	CREATED:	GENRE:
106M+	14/2/2016	RPG

As a runner character in Freeze Tag, you must keep away from the Tagger, who has to tag everyone and turn them into ice before the timer ticks down to zero! You can become unthawed and have 'instant thaw' powers, but when these run out you'll need to purchase more. You are told what your personal boosts are before each game, which is handy. Most characters try to find a decent hiding spot on the map and hope the Tagger doesn't locate them, but your boosts will be needed to get you out of a frozen mess. Invincibility boosts are always a joy to have!

Connor VIII has a history of great updates for Freeze Tag. At the start of 2020 he updated the 'cool' new ArcticCitadel map and castle, added new chat game tags and even brought back the Airport map. Before this, the new lobby came with three new obstacle courses, so there are always reasons to keep going back to this chilled out adventure!

COOL SHADES

- DID YOU KNOW? -

Freeze Tag collected 10,000 concurrent players for the first time in January 2020.

KEEP MOVING!

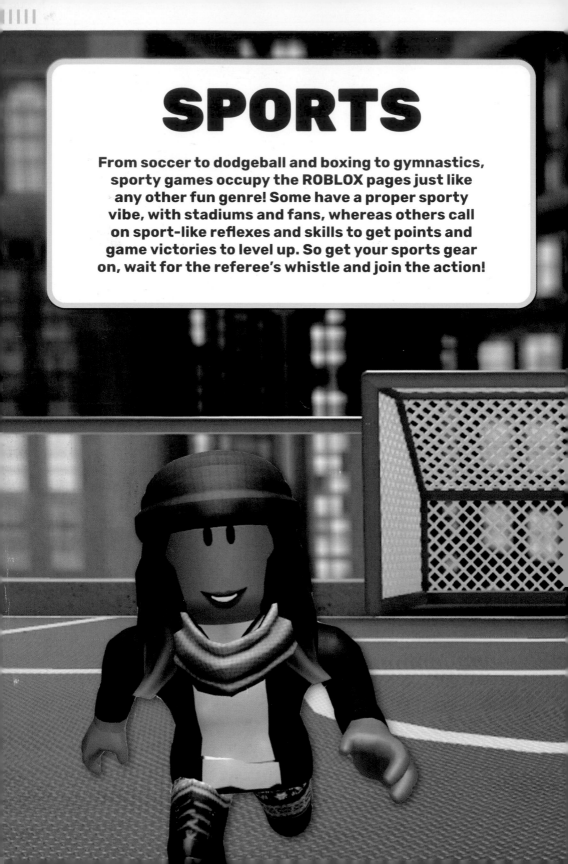

SPORTS

From soccer to dodgeball and boxing to gymnastics, sporty games occupy the ROBLOX pages just like any other fun genre! Some have a proper sporty vibe, with stadiums and fans, whereas others call on sport-like reflexes and skills to get points and game victories to level up. So get your sports gear on, wait for the referee's whistle and join the action!

LEGENDS OF SPEED

56

Pretty much all sports games need you to be quick on your feet, but that's taken to a completely new level in Legends of Speed! With nearly 400 million visits racked up within 12 months of its release, this is actually one of the fastest-growing games ever. Mixing sports with tactics, adventure and a high level of trading and rewards, LOS just has to be given a go!

The sporting goal in Legends of Speed is to be the quickest player on the map. The pre-game lobby area is really useful and can keep you busy for hours. Here, you can practise your running skills and begin to pick up coloured orbs and steps, which ultimately lead to you being faster. Different orbs have different stats!

by **Scriptbloxian Studios**

QUICK STATS

👍 BEST GAMES RATING: **91%**

VISITS: 390M+

CREATED: 22/4/2019

GENRE: Sports

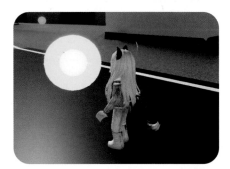

PRACTICE MAKES PERFECT

Time your runs to take in the speed ramps and you'll see your stats sky rocket! Use the ramps to leap through hoops in the air, and even slide off tower blocks for even bigger bonuses. When your speed, exp and level status have improved, click accept for a real race!

Races spawn in locations like desert, grassland and magma. Players line up at the start, then have to dash through the course to pick up either a gold, silver or bronze finish. At rookie (default) level you won't be winning any medals, but stick at it and keep leveling up and you'll soon be a speedy sports star winning races galore! When racing, look up as well as in front of you for the hoops and floating islands.

After your first rebirth you can begin trading with other players and use the shop to cash in on the gems and boosts that you have. You can also purchase passes and packs. Spend some time in this sporty arena and you won't be surprised to see users with a one million plus steps and over 50 race wins to their name!

- DID YOU KNOW? -

If you join the Scriptbloxian Studios community group, you can qualify for special rewards around the lobby!

WHOOSH!

ON YOUR MARKS...

55 DODGE**BALL!**

Schools and teams all around the world play dodgeball – the action-packed sport of throwing soft balls at another team with the aim of eliminating their players before your team is wiped out. Sounds cool, hey? And if you need another reason to jump in and join the ROBLOX game of Dodgeball!, it's made by alexnewtron – the hero in charge of MeepCity!

Dodgeball! rules are straightforward and no technical details are needed. You join either the red or blue team, and when you enter the court you try to throw your balls to strike the other players. Games are six-a-side and you must remain in your half of the court. You'll see how well you're doing by the

by alexnewtron

QUICK STATS

👍 BEST GAMES **RATING:** **80%**

VISITS: 56M+　　CREATED: 2/3/2015　　GENRE: Sports

heart-shaped symbol on your screen. If this drops, it means you're taking damage and you should do all you can to last the match. Taking refuge at the back of the court is sensible, and keep moving and jumping to make yourself harder to hit. Never turn your back on the opposition as you won't be able to spot the flying objects coming your way. Remember, too, that being struck on any part of your body counts as a hit.

YOU CAN'T DODGE ME!

LEVEL 1

YOU ARE OUT!

Play will come down to sudden death when one side has just a single player remaining – it then becomes a scramble to dodge the balls as they'll all be aimed at one person! Knockouts (KOs) hits and throw stats are recorded and an MVP is always declared. The sportiness is ramped up by being awarded levels. Getting XP, or buying items that can auto boost your XP, will also see you progress through the ranks.

Cool Dodgeball! skins are available in the shop, ranging from basketballs to bowling balls, and even scary eyeball skins! You need Certz, the in-game currency, to give yourself a fresh and standout look from the shop. Noob players can be easy to spot in Dodgeball!, so learn quickly to help your team to survive the madness after the starting whistle blows!

54 KICK OFF

Kick Off keeps clocking up the visits, with tens of millions returning each year for a sporty spectacle. It doesn't need constant updates and hyping from the ROBLOX Games page, because this game is so simple and effective, with addictive scoring and a stylish GUI (graphical user interface).

Soccer games are played in five v five matches, with the pitches located in a range of weird and wacky places, including dusty fields, urban environments and chilly Arctic pitches with igloos on the side! You'll play as either team USA or Brazil, and it's essential that you get to grips ASAP with the hotkeys and configurations for whatever platform you're playing on.

by **CM Games**

QUICK STATS

👍 BEST GAMES **RATING:** **82%**

VISITS: 205M+

CREATED: 11/11/2015

GENRE: Sports

- DID YOU KNOW? -

Kick Off has been ticked as a favourite over 1 million times, which is impressive for a sports game!

SHOOT

It can be tricky to see what's going on in the game, so try zooming out for a wide angle view to see more of the on-pitch action and the position of your teammates. There's no minimap option to display this! In order to score, you'll need to block, pass and run with the ball. Power, trickshot and stamina bars are displayed on screen – if you sprint a lot to chase the opposition, your stamina level will need time to recharge. A spinning trickshot stunt is a fab way to stick the ball in the net and will leave the others looking gob smacked!

Kick Off is quite stat heavy and you should pay attention to the lists of goals and passes displayed in the lobby area as well as on the leaderboard during games. As the clock counts down, make sure that you help your team to put pressure on the other's defense and ensure that the keeper is busy! Another individual award is to pick up the MVP prize for top soccer star after each match. Reckon you can do it? Of course you can!

During intermission and while servers load, head out from the lobby for a practice kick-about with the giant soccer ball on the small turfed area. This will help you hone your skills, and have a laugh too! In the lobby, hover over the other players to spy in their individual stats, including the distances they have netted from.

TAKE THE SHOT!

SUPER STRIKER LEAGUE

53

by **Cinder Studio**

Following on from Kick Off on the previous page, Super Striker League shows what can happen if you take a popular and simple sports game idea and ramp it up to the extreme! SSL grabbed nearly 30 million visits in just over six months since launch. The ROBLOX community took to the game so quickly that the developers were awarded the Builderman Award at the 2020 Bloxys!

QUICK STATS

👍 BEST GAMES **RATING: 81%**

VISITS:	CREATED:	GENRE:
29M+	24/6/2019	Sports

Unlike Kick Off, SSL allows players to unlock different items and grab upgrades to make them a better player on the soccer pitch. These include invincibility stars, boosts and bombs. Once inside the glitzy Striker City, the teleporter takes you away to a random pitch where crazy games take place at super speeds. Games are quick and skillful – just watch out for unexpected interruptions such as laser machines knocking you over!

XP, cash and points are all on offer in each game and you can rank yourself against the very best via the leaderboards. If you become a true elite sportsman, you may even make the Player of the Day accolade! Use the supercharge function to blast towards the goal, and the kicks with increased charge will stun and shock the opposition.

Keep coming back to Super Striker League to collect cash through the daily reward spin. Once you're comfortable with the mechanics and know how to master a match alongside your teammates, why not set up a private match with party members and friends?

SUPER STRIKER!

BOXING SIMULATOR

52

by **Tetra Games**

Can you duck and dive, train hard and roll with the punches? Boxing Simulator is a sports and role-playing hybrid game, allowing you to take on the character of a powerful and skillful athlete and train to become the best in the sport. It's a tough test and requires a tough personality!

QUICK STATS

👍 BEST GAMES **RATING: 85%**

VISITS:	CREATED:	GENRE:
37M+	6/10/2019	Sports

It's fun when you join the game and see yourself with giant gloves! As part of your routine, start by heading to the daily rewards area. Here, you can scoop up free coins, and scattered around the islands are many more coins that can be added to your stash. Boxing Simulator has lots of trading options, boosting your powers and strength. Strength can be sold in the shop and your DNA can be upgraded as well. New players are ranked as 'Noob' boxers, so you'll want to improve on this and build up to Rookie, Intermediate and higher. The last thing you want is other athletes to think you're weak!

Enter the boxing rings for one-on-one duels against other fighters, but try to have as many tricks up your sleeve as possible, such as x2 swing speed to put the frighteners on your foes! As you progress you'll become exposed to different opponents (watch out for the monsters in the dungeons!) and as a treat, you may fancy unlocking pets using the gems you've collected. Boxing Simulator packs quite a punch and everything won't be as it seems!

- DID YOU KNOW? -

Boxing Simulator 2 is also available from the Games page, but the original usually has more concurrent players and busier matches.

PUT 'EM UP!

GYMNASTICS GYMNASIUM

51

by **Olympic Gymnast Competition**

If your avatar wants to get super fit and learn some neat routines, twists and turns with as many as 85 other users, then swing by the Gymnastics Gymnasium! It's a sports extravaganza, full of good-natured competition with a variety of classic gymnastic sports and equipment.

QUICK STATS

👍 BEST GAMES **RATING: 86%**

VISITS: 32M+ **CREATED:** 18/12/2016 **GENRE:** Sports

The activities involved include floor, uneven bars, horizontal bars, pommel horse, balance, rings and more. You can use the open mat areas and lanes to perform and practise your own routines. In Gymnastics Gymnasium, there are rules to follow such as waiting your turn and being mindful of others, because the floor is busy. Take note of the four competitive levels on offer, starting at novice, then intermediate, advanced and elite. Gymnasts will remain in their appropriate level until their skill and experience increases.

The spectate mode is a clever way to watch more experienced performers on the equipment and to pick up top tips. Sprinting and flipping from a springboard may seem simple enough,

but the pros make it look effortless! Whatever platform you're on, joining the equipment and carrying out a move is a simple mouse click or button press away. Try to remember the key movements so that you become more free-flowing on the apparatus. Fun events and monthly competitions will boost your abilities and fine-tune your performances under pressure. Above all, though, have fun in this super sporty arena!

- DID YOU KNOW? -

Users can design their own leotards or purchase others in Gymnastics Gymnasium.

SWOOSH!

10/10!

50 HOCKEY WORLD

by **Hockey World**

When the puck drops, you better be ready for a super showdown on the ice! Hockey World takes you to the heart of the ice hockey arena, where high-speed dashes, bashes and smashes of the stick against the puck determine who comes out on top and who will be left decked out on the floor with a freezing face!

QUICK STATS

👍 BEST GAMES **RATING: 81%**

VISITS:	CREATED:	GENRE:
1.7M+	15/2/2019	Sports

As a new player, first teleport to a practice server for some one-on-one play. This will help you adjust to using your stick, tackling and going for goal – there is a goalkeeper (goaltender) in the net, so scoring won't be a complete doddle! Just like in high profile NHL games, there's a physical edge out there on the ice, so stay strong along with your teammates and focus on tackling, quick passing and a direct passage to the net.

Learn how to power up your stick to take maximum shots in the three v three league games. Goals and assists can be purchased in the lobby area, as well as custom goal songs and stick customizations to lend an individual edge to your sporty style on the ice.

- DID YOU KNOW? -

The locker rooms have inspirational phrases on the walls, such as 'Never Give Up', which proves that ice hockey is a tough sport!

WHACK!

FIGHTING

Let's get ready to rumbleeee! Millions of gamers get to grips with fighting games in ROBLOX, from scrapping with scary monsters to close-up combat with opponents using weapons, fists and feet. Fighting games crossover into FPS, Adventure and Horror, but whatever the style of the title you can be sure of one thing... it's a fight that you must win!

HEROES ONLINE

49

Spinning strike, whirlwind kick and ferocious uppercut are all sick special moves you can master in Heroes Online! For fighting game fans, this popular adventure is a must-play. As well as the fierce combat on offer, there's the chance to upgrade your powers and accept crucial quests. Have you got what it takes to become a hero?

You'll spawn first in Hosu City, as further game modes like team battles and the Beast's Forest can only be unlocked as you reach higher levels. Get the right look for your superhero fighting character by detailed editing, including clothing, hair, eyes and skin colour. Meet the guides around the map and accept missions from them. Taking on a simple sparring task early

by **Bloxxit Studios**

QUICK STATS

👍 BEST GAMES **RATING: 89%**

VISITS: | CREATED: | GENRE:
80M+ | 22/6/2018 | Fighting

- DID YOU KNOW? -

The team battle mode is an intense five-v-five situation that you scrap to come out of on top spot!

FIND THE ACTION!

on allows you to try out your hand-to-hand combat skills. Your quest status is displayed on screen and you complete it to earn yen, XP and fame points for future upgrades.

In Heroes Online, powers are known as quirks. When you've defeated enemies and finished tasks, quirks can be equipped to a slot you can easily use in fights (keys: e, r, t, f, or g on a keyboard) to increase your fighting efficiency. Quirks are sorted into common, rare, epic and legendary status, with the higher end quirks offering much more power. Unleash a mix of kicks and punches on your opponent to finish them off quickly!

A cool part of Heroes Online are the graphics, with the screen shaking during fighting for an epic experience. Clashes with opponents see comic-style animation but it's still easy to watch your health and energy status, which is a key thing during fights.

Keep reaching new levels and soon you'll be invited to an event, such as Rescue the Civilians. In this scenario you'll have a limited time to find and help innocent people around the map, again in return for a boost to yen and XP, as well as SP levels. Keep progressing and eventually you'll master team combats and take on bosses for huge prizes!

48 RO-GHOUL

by SushiWalrus

No, you haven't accidentally opened the horror game pages! Ro-Ghoul is a beastly fighting and adventure game, with plenty of on-screen shocks and surprises to keep you fixated on the battles and characters involved. Like many traditional fighting games there's plenty of punching, kicking, blocking and attacking involved, as well as the added bonus of weapons, collecting materials and completing tasks.

In the world of Ro-Ghoul, which is heavily influenced by Japanese anime, you become a valued member of the CCG that must track down and take out evil ghouls. People must be protected from these creepy creatures, which is easier said than done as ghouls are monsters that can appear very similar to regular people! To fight them off, the CCG is

QUICK STATS

👍 BEST GAMES **RATING:** **84%**

VISITS:	CREATED:	GENRE:
423M+	12/7/2017	Fighting

armed with weapons called quinques. Quinques have similar properties to the ghouls' weapons, which are known as kagunes.

Be sure to hide your identity when you're out fighting by wearing a mask as this will help shield your character from harmful revenge attacks from the ghouls. RC cells are a very vital ingredient in Ro-Ghoul. These are the building blocks for the quinque weapons, and the RC cells you harvest can be sent to CCG headquarters.

LOOK AT THAT VIEW

Doing this allows you to upgrade your lethal weapons and become a more effective fighter! Tasks can also be carried out for the CCG and as a reward your reputation status will improve.

On keyboards, evade moves can be achieved by double tapping the W, A, S, D keys. Use X to toggle sprint and Q to strike out. Landing hits will give you experience points and you should try to pay attention to your focus stats, too. Use these to increase your physical powers, such as punch strength and dash distance, and also directly boosting your quinques' capabilities.

The team aspect of Ro-Ghouls comes into play as well. You can form allies and bond as a team, meaning others won't fight you. But, if you try to friend someone who doesn't want to be, the decision may backfire! So, good luck as you take on the ghastly ghouls!

47 BLOX **FRUITS**

Blox Fruits doesn't sound like a typical fighting game, but don't be fooled into thinking that just because of the quirky name, it's only harmless food-based fun! Blox Fruits, which was actually originally called Blox Piece until the summer of 2019, combines fighting, quests and action adventures in a game with many outcomes and twists.

Blox Fruits kicks off by asking users to choose their side. This is either the good side of the Marines or the evil Pirates, and going on a journey with their chosen side. Firstly you'll enter the safe zone, where player-versus-player damage is disabled and users face the automated fighters in the

by go play eclipsis

QUICK STATS

👍 BEST GAMES **RATING:** **93%**

VISITS: 325M+   CREATED: 16/1/2019   GENRE: Fighting

x
- DID YOU KNOW? -

Fighters can switch teams at any point in a game by going to one of the recruiters positioned around the islands.

BOOST YOUR LEVELS!

game. In order to boost your levels, taking on a quest to defeat trainees will reward you with Beli, the in-game currency, and exp points. Typically an early-level defeat will pocket you around 40 Beli and 36 exp through melee (close-up combat) victories in a particular quest.

A fighter's health and energy levels are indicated on screen through the green and blue indicators. To move swiftly around the map and dash between fights, players can use the dash hotkey (which is 'q' on PC) but keep in mind that dashing zaps your energy. While you rest, though, energy levels regenerate. Sprinting is also an option, which is enabled through the 'control' button for keyboard players. For users on mobiles,

the developers recommend setting the 'fast mode' option so that lag is reduced as much as possible.

Once you've leveled up and visited key characters such as the Sword Dealer, Blox Fruit players can sail away to new islands and fight against new enemies. When you reach a new destination, remember to set your spawn location there so that when you're eliminated, you can be reinstated in that zone and not go back to the complete beginning.

The hand-to-hand combat is animated really well in the game, with cartoon-like damage stats flying from characters as you swing and strike away. Personal fighting stats can also be set depending on the type of destroyer you are.

TAKE A WALK

LOOK AT ME!

46 SUPER DOOMSPIRE

by **doomsquires**

For an explosive twist, check out the fighting and battles going on in the Super Doomspire world! Less of a close-up duel and faceoff compared to some games in this genre, it still offers plenty of punch, power and excitement as you compete alongside your teammates for victory.

QUICK STATS

BEST GAMES **RATING: 81%**

VISITS: 14M+ **CREATED:** 24/8/2019 **GENRE:** Fighting

The basic goal is to destroy the coloured towers of opposing teams before they can do the same to yours. Whether you join the yellow, green, red or blue side, you're instructed to destroy all spawns and eliminate all players to claim the win. You have weapons at your disposal to do this. The rocket launcher looks menacing and can help take down towers, as well as transporting you to another team's location. It's ideal in short and long range attacks. The bomb can help you jump high and break up towers, although it can be difficult to target your attacks precisely. Other weapons include the sword, trowel and superball. Superballs have the ability to

be supercharged for increased impact, so spend some time mastering exactly how to serve up these giant tennis ball-like projectiles!

If your team wins and overcomes the other spires, your knockout (KO) stats, as well as spawn and kill death ratio, will be displayed and you can equip new upgrades. In the stats breakdown, fighters can also check over their numbers for bricks, reflects and fallout KOs.

- DID YOU KNOW? -

Tasks are graded in beginner, intermediate and advanced level.

THIS IS THE ONE!

SWORD FIGHTING TOURNAMENT

by TheGamer101

45

Don't forget to keep checking in on the games that were released **TWO DECADES** ago! Yup, Sword Fighting Tournament was first unleashed in 2009, but thanks to some handy updates from the developer The Gamer101, it's still a tasty fighting game with plenty to keep you on your guard!

The developers describe it as ROBLOX's most popular sword fighting game. You have the powers to battle random enemy players, or your friends, in a range of game modes and tournaments. The choice of swords on offer is impressive, and coupled with the interesting maps and locations, you have the perfect mix of tools and terrains to take on a challenge. Games can be one-on-one matchups or more chaotic free-for-alls. Take them seriously, though, as you'll pick up badges and eventually you can work towards the super badge! Display this medal of honour in Sword Fighting Tournament and the powerful free energy sword will be yours.

QUICK STATS

👍 **BEST GAMES RATING: 83%**

VISITS: 45M+ **CREATED:** 12/8/2009 **GENRE:** Fighting

- DID YOU KNOW? -

Different swords deal different damage and can be used at varying ranges.

On some maps, staying on the low ground is the best tactic for unleashing your weapon, but there is the potential to launch a surprise attack as opponents move to reach higher spots. Hiding and surprising opponents is a classic caper. Be aware of maps with areas that move and don't get stuck down a dead end – it could spell the end of your tournament!

SWOOSH!

SWISH!

44 SABER SIMULATOR

by **HD Games**

Star Wars fanatics will enjoy this action-packed fighting game! Saber Simulator's rammed with weapon-based quests, and you'll get a mega rush from swooping and swooshing your saber to beef up your powers and status. It's all about the best tools you can earn and equip! With over 250 million visits in just five months since hitting the ROBLOX front page, expect Saber Simulator to be around for a long time and get better and better with cool updates from the HD Games gang.

QUICK STATS

👍 BEST GAMES **RATING: 88%**

VISITS: 275M+ **CREATED:** 7/9/2019 **GENRE:** Fighting

coins. These precious coins allow you to upgrade your saber, plus your DNA and fighting class. After all, you don't want to stay as a noob-level character for too long – the class of soldier, overlord, demigod and cerberus sounds much more frightening to your foes!

Training your character and swinging your saber keeps your strength status rising. Having increased strength boosts your health and damage levels to a mark that makes you a real handful to hold back in a duel. Keep training and soon you can trade your strength for

Unlocking saber levels will lead to a dramatic rise in your powers, with the green 2x saber the first upgrade you should aim for. The ultimate aim is to become the only player on the top of the hill – this awards you a king point and you can begin your royal reign on the leaderboard!

- DID YOU KNOW? -

Pets are part of Saber Simulator and they can be leveled up and equipped too!

UNLOCK LEVELS!

43 APOCALYPSE RISING

by Gusmanak

Even though this classic ROBLOX game has an official creation date of 1 April, there are zero pranks and jokes involved! Apocalypse Rising is a deadly serious situation where survival and fighting off zombies is crucial. It combines fighting, adventure, weapons, tactics... and some serious sprinting to safety!

QUICK STATS

BEST GAMES **RATING: 90%**

VISITS: 215M+ | CREATED: 1/4/2008 | GENRE: Fighting

The maps in Apocalypse Rising are huge, with both the Reborn and Hardcore zones covering 19 square km and offering a vast landscape for exploration and adventure. Users need to get by in the wasteland by picking up the scattered food and drinks. This will replenish your thirst and hunger levels, which must be maintained so that you have the energy to fight back and escape from the waves of zombies.

Select a perk from cardio (double speed and stamina), survivalist (extra thirst and hunger levels), ninja (stealth) and vitality (health) and hit the spawn button. Semi auto weapons have limited mag size and will take a few seconds to reload, so use your ammo sparingly as you progress through the map and fend off the cruel creatures. Watch your levels at the bottom of the screen as sprinting around zaps energy from you.

Your inventory capacity can be bolstered and prepare you better for a scrap with the monsters. Try to master moving building equipment and pieces to help you stay alive in the zones – the screen will inform you of when other players are eliminated, so you don't want your name joining them!

ARG!

HE'S BEHIND YOU!

BATTLE ROYALE

This game genre has become super popular in recent years! Gamers can drop on an island and start scavenging and looting for weapons and items, with the target being to remain as the last player after eliminating your enemies. Battle royale adventures are fun, frantic and packed with pulsating possibilities!

42

ALONE:
BATTLE ROYALE

Based on the monstrously popular Fortnite Battle Royale computer game, Alone takes you into a map full of adventure and weaponry with a very similar style. The mission is to be the last person left in the game! The only major thing that Alone doesn't have compared to Fortnite is the ability to build.

Players start by choosing between a duo, solo or squad battle royale game in the lobby. There are often limited time offers to tempt you with any spare Robux you may have, such as starter pack crates, and you can also visit the store for epic upgrades and items. Alone also has an hourly item that cycles through the store.

by **Clockwork Entertainment**

QUICK STATS

👍 BEST GAMES **RATING: 90%**

VISITS: **32M+** CREATED: **15/2/2019** GENRE: **Battle Royale**

x
- DID YOU KNOW? -

As many as 64 players can land on the map at the same time!

x
WHERE WILL YOU LAND?

Players (either as a team or individual), are then teleported to the plane for a sky dive onto the map. Watch where other players head to because (as you drop with no weapons) you'll need to look for loot so that you can stock up on weapons and ammo to strike first. Places to loot and hide out in include the farm, hospital, factory, chapel and docks. Stock up your arsenal and begin to aim down your sights to take shots at the enemy. You won't be able to just stay on the edge of the map though, because the storm will move in, forcing players to face up to each other as you remain in the scary circle!

Players can operate in first person or third person mode and keep an eye on the clock ticking down and the number of battle royale players left in action, plus your own kill count. Use med kits and bandages to heal, if you've picked them up, and when you're in team play you should keep communicating so that your tactics are clear as you chase a squad win.

If your armour and health status holds out and you're down to the final two players, try lining up a shot from a distance or throwing in a grenade as a final act to eliminate the enemy and for you to become the royale champion!

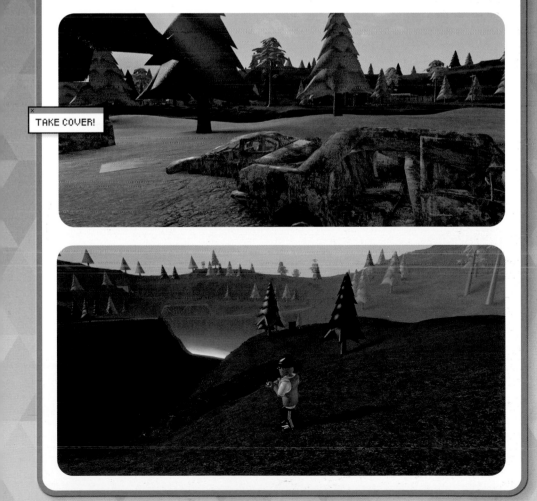

41 ISLAND **ROYALE**

The stats are very impressive for Island Royale! In just two years, as the battle royale mode exploded thanks to the success of Fortnite, the ROBLOX game has reached over 300 million visits and has been liked 1.2 million times. It's a great version of the video game and, unlike Alone Battle Royale, it does include the ability to build and craft defences such as walls and towers.

With as many as 200 players active on a server, the island is a very busy place to play! Solo, duo and squad games can be picked from the lobby area, as well as special modes such as flood, zone wars, TDM (team deathmatch), and FFA (free-for-all). The arena mode can only be entered once a player has reached a

by LordJurrd

QUICK STATS

👍 BEST GAMES **RATING:** **90%**

VISITS: 310M+

CREATED: 8/1/2018

GENRE: Battle Royale

- DID YOU KNOW? -

If you're eliminated, you can stay spectating the person who took you out so that you can pick up some battle royale tips.

YOU CAN BE THE LAST ONE STANDING!

THINK
TACTICALLY

certain rank. The lobby is also the place to access the shop where cool gliders, tools, clothing, hats, emotes, win and death effects can all be bought with the in-game Bucks currency.

Deploy to the island, drop from the bus and begin the quest to become the last player, or team, remaining. One other difference to Alone Battle Royale is that fighters don't need to loot for weapons when they drop, with cool equipment like pistols, assault rifles and shotguns already loaded in your slots. New weapons and items can be collected around the map and picked up from eliminated players.

Your character spawns with a supply of materials too, which are wood, brick and metal. Elite players quickly learn how to make forts and ramps as this gives them the high ground, and the best sniping point, over advancing enemies.

Your shield and health bar levels are key to your survival, so think carefully before you venture over open land as you could be picked off and eliminated with a simple single shot. You'll be placed on the match end leaderboard, alongside the kills you make in the game.

DEADLOCKED BATTLE ROYALE

40

by Mega Drive

Deadlocked Battle Royale is home to as many as 50 players, all looking for that one thing... to be the final fighter standing! It's an easy game for battle royale beginners to play, with simple controls and instructions but also a fun game user interface with lots of addictive measures. So, get out on the island and go for that vital victory!

QUICK STATS

👍 BEST GAMES **RATING: 82%**

VISITS: 24M+   **CREATED:** 2/4/2018   **GENRE:** Battle Royale

There are five game modes to choose from, with the regulars of solo, duo and squad joined by two further fun options. Gamers can opt in for a big 25 v 25 battle royale, where chaos reigns as the two big teams try to wipe each other out, as well as the playground choice. Playground is where you can hone and perfect your battle royale skills for 60 minutes, including how to build and equip weapons. You can raid boxes and fill up your inventory with a host of powerful guns, all without the

threat of coming under a real attack. Spend time becoming familiar with the functions and how to toggle between the six slots at your fingertips.

Building materials are called reinforced wood and stone and, in regular game modes, these can be harvested by using your tool to grind at trees and objects. Bandages and med kits are essential in a combat. So after taking any damage find a shielded spot to heal yourself. Weather, too, plays a role in Deadlocked Battle Royale. Be sure to stay out of the lightning showers!

DROP ME IN!

BATTLE ROYALE
SIMULATOR

by **XS Dev**

Battle Royale Simulator has so much to offer in this game genre. Despite having the word 'simulator' in its title, this adventure still feels very complete when compared to other games, and even has a few twists that others don't. Time to load it up and give it a go!

QUICK STATS

👍 BEST GAMES **RATING: 83%**

VISITS:	CREATED:	GENRE:
24M+	8/3/2019	Battle Royale

Battle Royale Simulator is quick and easy to get started. There's no waiting in the lobby for teammates to join you, as you can drop in on a game at any time. This means that when you deploy from the bus over the island, there will already be battles in place on the ground – as you swoop in take a look around to see any combat hotspots and tracer fire whipping around! This does mean that players can shoot at you before you land, so be ready to react and change your route down to the ground if needed. Games just keep continuing and there's no storm shrinking, but you'll want to impress

and pick up the most kills as possible to boost your KDR figure and position on the overall leaderboard. Bucks are awarded for each elimination you make and these can be exchanged for ace items and upgrades in the shop.

Use the bounce pads around the map to fling you into the air and away from danger, where you can also redeploy your glider to bring you back down. Cool golf buggies can be driven, too, and this is a great tactic for fleeing from danger. Raid chests to better weapons, like rocket launchers and sniper rifles, and use the bandages to heal yourself and prepare for the next deadly duel!

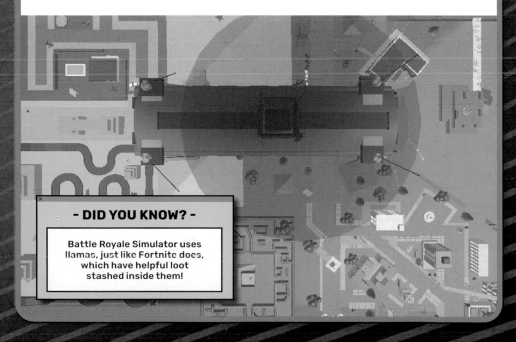

- DID YOU KNOW? -

Battle Royale Simulator uses llamas, just like Fortnite does, which have helpful loot stashed inside them!

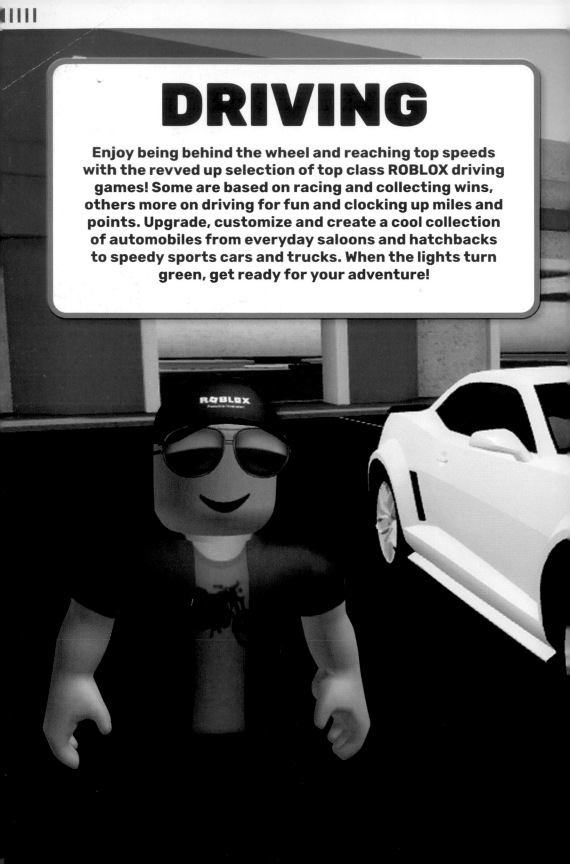

DRIVING

Enjoy being behind the wheel and reaching top speeds with the revved up selection of top class ROBLOX driving games! Some are based on racing and collecting wins, others more on driving for fun and clocking up miles and points. Upgrade, customize and create a cool collection of automobiles from everyday saloons and hatchbacks to speedy sports cars and trucks. When the lights turn green, get ready for your adventure!

38 VEHICLE SIMULATOR

Speeding into pole position as an awesome racing, driving and RPG-type game, Vehicle Simulator has something for every ROBLOX fan! Even if you're not a keen car person, Vehicle Simulator has hours of gameplay action and if four-wheeled machines aren't your thing, remember that you can also take charge of planes and boats!

There's a very stylish look to this racing sim. Use your onscreen mobile phone to gather essential info and search for your favourite vehicles. You must select from several roles at the beginning of the game – tow trucker, police officer, citizen, SWAT officer, transit driver and prisoner – with citizen advised as the best way to ease beginners in. Some roles are

by Simbuilder

QUICK STATS

👍 BEST GAMES **RATING: 90%**

VISITS: 445M+

CREATED: 8/8/2014

GENRE: Driving

- DID YOU KNOW? -

In March 2020, Vehicle Simulator became available for mobile and tablet ROBLOX players for the first time, with 40,000 in-game cash also up for grabs!

VROOM! VROOM!

locked early on. Enter into a dealership and see what cars you can afford based on classes such as sport, comfort, special and truck. A vehicle's speed, acceleration, braking and handling stats are provided to help you decide.

Begin racing through the city and completing quests and tasks to pocket money. This will allow you to upgrade and fine tune your motors. Out in the streets, aim for top speed to see the cash pour in! Performing stunts, winning drag races and doing track laps are all beneficial. There are also badges to collect – 50 race wins awards you the track master and further badges are for being a globetrotter and road warrior.

Speaking of stunts, Vehicle Simulator regularly hooks up with toy makers Hot Wheels for official race events, where you can fly and zoom through the air doing stunts on miles of their classic orange tracks and loops!

The 3D map is a helpful sat nav tool for drivers as they negotiate busy maps. Plus don't forget to use the recording function to capture yourself behind the wheel in quality cinematic mode. Going for test drives in high speed cars before you buy them is awesome fun and if you're really aiming for the top, try out the new Bugatti Sharon for a slice of the hypercar lifestyle!

JUMP THE BRIDGE!

37

CAR CRUSHERS 2

Push the pedal to the floor, hit top gear and go cruising and crashing in this fun driving game! Car Crushers 2 is one of the most successful racing games in the history of ROBLOX, with loads of front seat action to keep you gripped to the wheel. It's a mix of speedy driving and tactical arena battles, so start up the ignition to start the madness!

For proper petrolheads, Car Crushers 2 allows you lots of time to look through the garage of cars available and to make your prized picks. In order to start banking some money, you must go to the dealership and look over the motors available. This is where vehicles spawn and at first you're limited to the free cars, which are typically low powered and range from

by Car crushers official group

QUICK STATS

👍 BEST GAMES **RATING:** **85%**

VISITS: 257M+ | CREATED: 11/2/2017 | GENRE: Driving

70 mph to 107 mph top speeds, until you have some cash to splash on a speedier selection. CC2 provides excellent replicas of real machines, ranging from a sensible Toyota Prius to a powerful Lamborghini!

Cars are referred to as crushers in this game, and instead of being responsible with these high-priced vehicles, you're encouraged to get out on the map and start crushing

HONK! HONK!

them to pick up money and tokens! New crushers will unlock as you progress through the levels. If you become stuck on the car's side, for example, just use the handy 'flip vehicle' button from the menu to set you straight again and onto the path of mayhem. The main map is called the facility, and watch out for huge events like lava explosions which can totally wreck your plans! You may need to head for the rescue helicopter before time runs out in order to escape.

Cars can be customized in the dealership, as long as you have the cash to do so, and make sure you pay a visit to the derby arena. Accessed through the lobby teleporter, here you can pocket more money by destroying other people's cars, all in front of a cheering car-razy crowd!

36 FULL **THROTTLE**

Get your racing suit on, grab your helmet and get to the garage to rev up this incredible driving game! Made by Horizon Entertainment team and called Horizon until 2018, Full Throttle is an epic example of a ROBLOX motoring adventure that takes car details very seriously.

by **Horizon Entertainment**

QUICK STATS

👍 BEST GAMES RATING: **88%**

VISITS: 14M+ **CREATED:** 31/8/2017 **GENRE:** Driving

Drivers spawn in the city and have the option of entering the showroom or the motor shop. Head to the showroom and begin to check out the monster collection of cars in Full Throttle. The stats and info on offer are unlike most other car games, from usual details like top speed and acceleration to weight, engine size, torque level and horse power. Money and XP is gained

by the time you spend behind the wheel. If you flick through the leaderboard, you'll see the money which elite drivers pull in can be several million and thousands of miles clocked up.

Other details in the game that put a smile on your face include being able to give your cars a fun nickname, having the option of smoke coming from the

HEAD TO THE SHOW ROOM

exhaust pipes and changing the cars from auto to manual for an increased driver experience. The map has ramps and hoops to navigate and you can pick up extra XP for cool drifts around corners – looking stylish and in control behind the wheel is all part of the game! Look out for notifications showing that gold, bronze or diamond crates have spawned too, because the first driver to locate it will bag a cool reward to use in the shop.

Customizing is great fun in Full Throttle. From camo or carbon fibre wraps to magical mods, sporty spoilers, new rims, bigger engines and reflective paint jobs, the list of auto shop upgrades seems endless! The list of badges on offer range from simple tokens like buying your first car, to more difficult achlevements such as bagging a million coins or meeting the game owner.

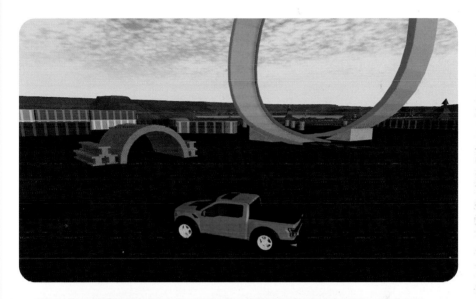

CHECK OUT THESE WHEELS!

35

ULTIMATE DRIVING: WESTOVER ISLANDS

by **TwentyTwo Pilots**

Join up to 27 other motoring mad fans on the same server and enjoy an epic four-wheeled adventure together. The TwentyTwo pilots group, who have over 50,000 ROBLOX followers, are legendary car game developers and with 119 million visits, Ultimate Driving: Westover Islands is their top-of-the-range attraction! It lets you race and explore with your friends across a vast map and with more than 100 lifelike cars to test out, grab the keys and get in the driver's seat.

QUICK STATS

👍 BEST GAMES **RATING: 86%**

VISITS: 119M+ | CREATED: 25/6/2011 | GENRE: Driving

Version four of UD: Westover Islands offers eight team selections, with most players opting for a trip to the Kensington, South Beach, Westover, Woodbury or Nomtauk locations at first. Drag and circuit racing is also available and so are the more slow-speed quests of driving buses or taxis

and delivering mail to houses. Driving, racing and doing the tasks needed in your job earn you XP and money, which you can spend on new cars and upgrades. Don't be too nervous driving a fast supercar, because the more expensive your machine the greater the driving rewards on offer!

The dealership and garage locations are the place to purchase and store your selection of slick autos. Although the cars don't have the official names, petrol heads will be able to recognize that Ferrari, Lambo, Porsche and McLaren replicas are all lined up on offer! Take your car into the customizing booths to add a little extra for a unique look around the roads.

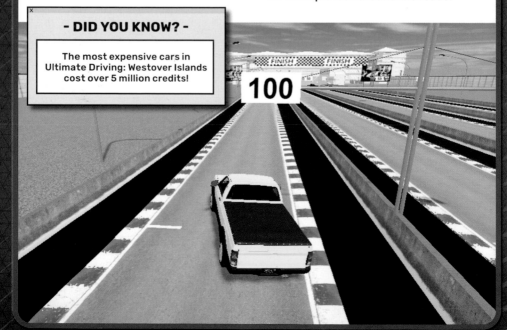

- DID YOU KNOW? -

The most expensive cars in Ultimate Driving: Westover Islands cost over 5 million credits!

100

CAR DEALERSHIP
TYCOON

by Foxzie's Productions

This is a car-based game with a bit of a tycoon twist! Instead of only racing around a mad map at supersonic speeds and taking on auto upgrades, players get the chance to launch their own dealership and rake in the big business bucks too!

QUICK STATS

👍 BEST GAMES **RATING: 90%**

VISITS: 75M+ **CREATED:** 27/3/2018 **GENRE:** Driving

Claim your piece of land and begin to decide what your dream dealership will look like. Getting cars equipped on your land and driving them around the streets will see your bank balance increase, which then means you can begin to plot your car sales empire. Platforms, walls, signs, furniture, sidewalks and more can be picked up from the item list and the more exciting cars you have on offer, the more cash will be coming to you!

Foxzie is obviously a big car fan because he keeps adding updated vehicles to the collection. The BMW M8, Porsche Taycan and McLaren P1 hyper car joined the ranks in a spring 2020 spectacular. It's not just speed demons, though, as the fearsome Dodge Ram truck and Mercedes G63 wagon also beefed up the car selling business in the recent updates. The map is also likely to change and new badge rewards give you even more incentives to keep the cash piling up from sales at the showroom!

Check out the speed, torque, handling and breaking data before you spawn your chosen vehicle and even though the streets are quiet in Car Dealership Tycoon, there's still the risk that you'll crash these high-powered cars and have to suffer the consequences!

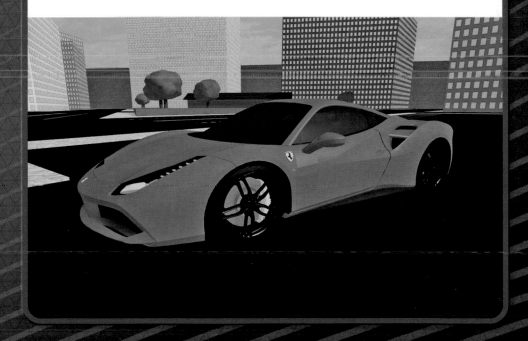

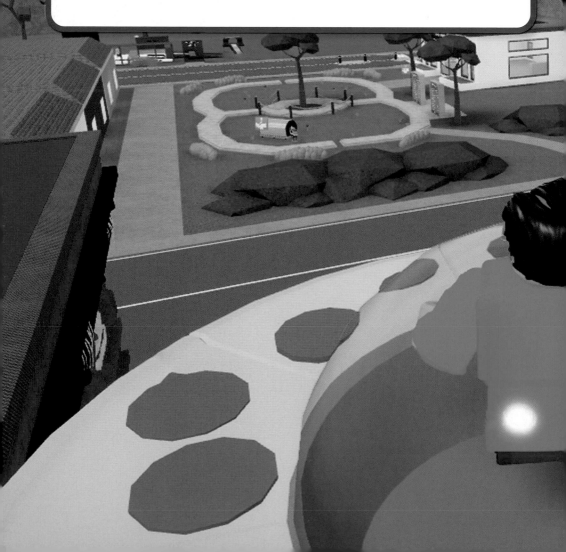

TYCOON GAMES

The tycoon genre doesn't exist by itself, with these money-making and business-led games being found in categories like building, town and city and RPG. If you enjoy making money, reaching goals and building up a company or successful factory, then you'll thrive on the unique demands and details that come with tycoon titles. Turn over to check out some of the very best!

SUPER HERO
TYCOON

33

Super Hero is one of the select ROBLOX games to join the billion plus visits club alongside such greats as Jailbreak and MeepCity. It's an incredible place to spend hours being creative and building up your tycoon business! You don't need to be a superhero super fan to enjoy this classic encounter... but it does help if you like having powers and acting as a caped crusader!

You'll spawn in the centre of the map and be faced with trying to claim a tycoon (land base) belonging to one of ten top heroes. These are The Flash, The Hulk, Black Panther, Batman, Iron Man, Superman, Ant-Man, Thor, Green

by **Super Heroes**

QUICK STATS

BEST GAMES **RATING:** **93%**

VISITS: 1.1B+ CREATED: 11/12/2016 GENRE: Super Heroes

- DID YOU KNOW? -

Dash over to the cash crates that drop and you can pick up even more money.

ZOOM!

Lantern and Spider-Man. To claim, simply run to the door of the tycoon and enter – the facility will then be yours! You can start admiring the place, staring around and dreaming of how to build it up, or you could do the sensible thing and begin raking in the big bucks quickly! To do this, go to the coloured icon and buy a dropper. You'll then see boxes drop on to your conveyor belt and, magically, the cash you earn will start appearing on your register inside your base. Awesome! To claim the money, simply stand by the register.

As your tycoon bank balance balloons, decide what to do with your building. When you have the funds, you can add walls to help protect your business from other heroes, and it's a good idea to place the security system over your entrance. Keep building up the walls, add further floors, staircases, lights and even more cool options! To keep the cash flowing, make sure you add more droppers and mega droppers to your production line. These will become more expensive, but the investment is worth it in the long run.

Outside of your tycoon, other super heroes will try to attack you. Watch out for gear crates dropping as these will reward you with a random weapon. Work on your shooting and combat technique to defend yourself and if you have spare Robux, placing turrets and a bunker outside your building will make you even more menacing!

TAKE WHAT YOU NEED!

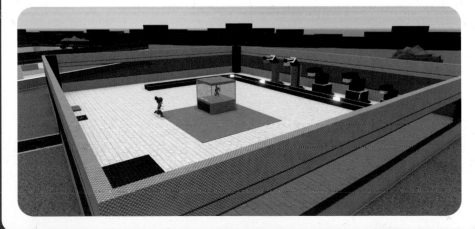

32 RESTAURANT TYCOON 2

Create, cook, serve and bank the money as you become an expert business operator in the world of restaurants! Can you make a fast buck from fast food, will you balance building and the roleplay tasks with keeping the customers happy and fed? Restaurant Tycoon 2 is perfect if you love eating up the profits! The original Restaurant Tycoon launched in 2017 and with over 330 million visits it's more popular over time, but more ROBLOXIANS come to the RT2 servers now, with as many 20,000 concurrent players!

by Ultraw

QUICK STATS	👍	BEST GAMES RATING: **89%**	
	VISITS: 143M+	**CREATED:** 1/7/2019	**GENRE:** Building

The gameplay is vast in Restaurant Tycoon 2. Start at level 1 by creating a new restaurant from five templates, then decide on the style of food you'd like to cook and sell. This can be from anywhere in the world – just check

- DID YOU KNOW? -

Empty or close your restaurant so that you can reorganize it to boost your cash flow!

out the handy onscreen guide to a country's cuisine and culture, which will defo get you licking your lips! Will it be hot dogs from the USA or fish and chips from the UK? You have the option of selecting a restaurant manager, then set about selecting chefs, waiters and operators from the non playable customer (NPC) list. Trainee chefs, for example, will need to watch you cook five meals before they qualify as a chef.

The key to collecting cash and cooking up a success in RT2 is to attract, sit and feed customers in your establishments. Using the upgrade options is very wise. This will allow you to advertise your restaurant around the map, select card payments from diners to speed up your workload and add a second floor to maximize revenue. Visits to the EKEA and construction store will help you develop your business. Be careful

to select the most cost effective equipment – you don't always need to spend extra money on a flashy designer table!

When you begin leveling you can collect fun extras like a car to tour the map and visit other places. Remember to keep your chefs and waiters happy though because if their happiness level drops and they're overworked, they won't level up as quickly. Also, always have a tip jar as a way to pocket more money!

- DID YOU KNOW? -

In happy hour, be sure to serve customers quickly so that you earn bonus cash before the day ends.

THEME PARK TYCOON 2

31

ROBLOX fans love a trip to the theme park! Theme Park Tycoon 2 allows you to build your own brilliant universe of rides and attractions, ranging from basic teacups to daredevil rollercoasters. But you must get the numbers and business side of the park correct for it to function – you need the cash to build and for the paying customers to keep on coming through those gates!

by Den_S

QUICK STATS	👍	BEST GAMES RATING:	**87%**
	VISITS: 345M+	**CREATED:** 2/1/2012	**GENRE:** Building

Claim your plot and start building. The mechanics and functions may seem hectic at first, so try using the tutorial button to get you started. Building is done in blocks, placing paths and rides in place as long as you have the money to do so. Get a small ride up and running right away to bring the crowds in – you'll need an entrance and exit and to then declare it open to earn those coins! Using the picker tool allows you to quickly repeat a build that you already have in your theme park as an easy way to boost earnings.

Be selective in your ride purchases and make choices that permit you to make the most from the smallest investment. Click on a ride's stats to see how it's

WHAT COOL RIDE WILL YOU BUILD FIRST?

performing and to read any thoughts that visitors leave. This will help you to improve the experience you offer. Visit other theme parks to get tips and see how they're built and operate. Luckily, the road around the map rapidly speeds you up while on foot!

Building is very stylish in Theme Park Tycoon and the detail will keep you busy for ages. Add stalls so that you can sell refreshments to boost your funds. Balancing the figures is a tricky task you'll need to master. You can increase the price of your attraction, but this may do damage long term as customers choose to stay away. Get your timing right as well – visitors want a ride that gives them satisfaction and value for money, but make them last too long and your profit will be damaged. Theme Park 2 is a game you'll want to save over a long time as you work towards becoming the very best in the business!

PIZZA FACTORY
TYCOON

by Ultraw

30

Extra cheese? Hot sauce? What will the toppings be on the pizzas you dish up in this exciting tycoon title? One thing's for sure – your mouth will be watering for tasty snacks just a few minutes after you tuck into this hugely popular tycoon-role-playing game!

QUICK STATS

BEST GAMES
RATING: 85%

VISITS: | CREATED: | GENRE:
390M+ | 2/8/2016 | Tycoon

Players start as a rookie cook, but don't waste any time in starting up your perfect pizza place. The priority is to get the production line going, with delicious bases dropping out and ready to be packed by you. Click on the fresh food and you'll earn 50 bucks, but as you develop your equipment this will rise to over 100 per pizza – sweet deal, hey! The building bit can now start to take place. Just simply step on the red buttons and purchase walls, windows, counters, menus, seats and more (if you have the cash). Make sure that you get a chef called a pizza clicker, to earn you cash while you're not in the factory!

Your rookie status will improve and soon customers will be coming to your business. Become a supreme baker and you can invent new pizzas after shopping for ingredients. After a while you'll be totally bossing the pizza scene! You'll need to keep the visitors happy in order to get a good rating! Add cashiers, which start from 5,000 bucks, to earn even more money.

- DID YOU KNOW? -

You can put helpful pizza-making gear in your factory, like a base cutter and cheese adder.

- DID YOU KNOW? -

Developer Ultraw is the clever dude behind the Restaurant Tycoon and Clone Tycoon games too!

EXTRA
TERRESTRIAL
TOPPINGS!

29

WORK AT A PIZZA PLACE

by **Dued1**

Continuing with the food theme, the famous Work at a Pizza Place game slots into several categories, from town and city to simulator and tycoon. It's packed with big 'slices' of action, and if you focus on the business side, players can get rewards for doing their jobs well and begin to build up their houses and items. The world of pizza making and delivering is an exciting one!

QUICK STATS

👍 BEST GAMES **RATING: 85%**

VISITS:	CREATED:	GENRE:
2.2B+	28/3/2008	Town & City

Select from cashier, cook, pizza boxer, deliver and supplier tycoon roles. Opt to work behind the restaurant's front desk and you're the person who takes orders from the customers. This should be straight forward and for each order you complete, you earn cash. You'll also get daily rewards and paychecks for completing your task. If you fancy a step up, hit the advanced button on the side of the restaurant to get more tricky questions and answers from the restaurant's visitors! Get things wrong and the other workers in the restaurant won't be happy.

Switch roles to packing pizzas and you'll earn moneyz, the in-game currency, for making the right orders and helping the team keep the restaurant working well. Cooking the food is a better way to make money and keep your bank balance looking as tasty as the treats you bake! You can also become the boss and take the manager's role when it becomes free. Just head for the manager's office and try to sit In the seat. Look after the workers, though, as they could turn against you in this business!

EXTRA CHEESE?

SIMULATOR GAMES

Do you like taking on a task, playing games, facing opponents and role-playing? Simulator games mix all of these skills and many more. There are hundreds of 'sim' titles to scan through on the ROBLOX games page. If you're a fan of taking on a challenge and competing to be the best that you can, with a slice of jeopardy and risk thrown in, then you'll enjoy the next five simulator games!

DESTRUCTION SIMULATOR

28

by **silky_dev**

QUICK STATS

👍 BEST GAMES **RATING:** **86%**

VISITS:	CREATED:	GENRE:
250M+	19/8/2018	Simulator

When a game wins a Bloxy award just a few months after its release, then you know you should check it out! Destruction Simulator smashed its way to the Favourite Breakout Game at the 2019 ceremony, beating other heavyweight sims such as Bee Swarm Simulator, Mining Simulator and Super Power Training Simulator to the title. Developer silky_dev has done a top job with this addictive sim!

As with all popular simulator games, Destruction Simulator has a basic idea that gets built on and expanded as you progress. Users start in the small lobby area at the beginning of the destruction zone and can

- DID YOU KNOW? -

There's a speedy track to take that whisks you away to the higher levels, rather than having to walk.

KABOOM!

only access the level 1 area. This is a racetrack setting and the aim, as with all destruction zones, is to blow up the landscape in return for bricks and coins. Basic, but brilliant fun! The mayhem is achieved by using your weapons to destroy the scenes, which are low level grenades and rocket launchers at first. You'll need to be an accurate shot and work out what destroyed objects reward you with the most bricks and money.

Other beginner players will also be in this level 1 area, so move quickly to zap the cars and stands and collect rewards before they can. Your backpack will fill with bricks and you can then sell or upgrade your stash. Sell and you'll swap it for precious coins, which can

then be used in the shop for superior rockets and bombs. This extra power will boost your damage capabilities and XP gathering. Don't forget to keep buying the best backpack that you can, too. Strapping on the camping pack or travel pack, when you can afford it, gives you extra capacity and means you can stay out in the destruction zones for longer.

Rockets such as the spy shooter and flamethrower have much quicker reload times, which means you're more efficient and dangerous at destroying. So save up your coins to collect a weapon that will really make you a standout star in this sim! If you move on to level 5 and higher and the equipment and buildings you can take down become a lot more complex and interesting.

MINING SIMULATOR

27

by **Rumble Studios**

The Builderman Award of Excellence Bloxy was handed out to Mining Simulator shortly after it launched. This fab sim dug new depths (sorry for the cheesy joke!) when it entered the Games page and with nearly 600 million visits in its first two years, gamers can't get enough of this underground adventure!

The basis is to mine below ground for different material blocks, called ores, and pick up coins to upgrade your avatar with much more effective tools and backpacks. You'll soon get tired of the default pickaxe and backpack, with their limited storage and time zapping functionality, and have your eyes on smart kits like the travel pack (2,000

QUICK STATS

👍 BEST GAMES **RATING: 90%**

VISITS: 592M+　**CREATED:** 10/2/2018　**GENRE:** Simulator

- DID YOU KNOW? -

Gamers who like playing the Minecraft game on consoles and PCs usually love the Mining Simulator game too.

storage) and the cylinder pack (200,000 storage). These beauties require at least 25,000 coins, though! The toxic pack in the rebirth shop requires 22,500 tokens but has a storage limit of 35 million. Wowsers!

If you mine basics like dirt and grass you'll collect a coin value of just 1. Target richer ores like copper, stone and obsidian and you'll scoop higher stakes. When your backpack is packed, just return to the top surface and sell your materials and buy new products.

A target to mine towards is 10 million coins. This will allow you to rebirth and double your ore value. Good idea, huh? Rebirthing is a cool function, but keep in mind that you sacrifice the backpacks,

tools and coins that you've built up. Check out the pets and hats upgrades as well. These items help to ramp up your mining speed and efficiency, plus the power and ore value. Hats can be picked up from crates or by trading with other players and will see your mining skills increased. Some hats even increase your jump power.

New players will become mates with Miner Mike, the helpful dude by the entrance to the mine. He has helpful quest instructions and tips and reminders for you, so follow his instructions to pick up boosts. Mining can be a lonely and dark simulator business, so you need all the friends you can get!

I'm Spaceman Steve

HI, SPACEMAN STEVE!

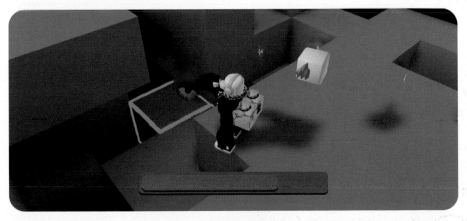

WEIGHT LIFTING SIMULATOR 3

26

Flamin' Studios call this the 'greatest training simulator of all time!' It's the perfect place to flex some serious muscle and make your body a bulging mass of strength. Showing off close to one billion visits and over two million likes in around just 18 months, Weight Simulator 3 is a powerhouse game for all simulator fans.

As you'd expect, you need to put in some serious time in the gym to make your avatar a muscly master. All characters begin as the stick class, which is a skinny character in need of big-time bulking up! To get bigger and reach the small fry rank, carry out the weightlift curls on your knees anywhere around the map. This gives

by Flamin' Studios

QUICK STATS

👍 BEST GAMES RATING: **87%**

VISITS: 945M+

CREATED: 12/9/2018

GENRE: Simulator

you between two to ten strength points and the next weight division is reached at 250. Carry on exercising and at 500 the press-up ability is unlocked and you'll be classed as a shrimp, followed by muscular (1,000), buff (2,500), tank (5,000), and monster (10,000). If you're really serious about upping your size and power, the legend rank is reached at a huge 80,000 strength points!

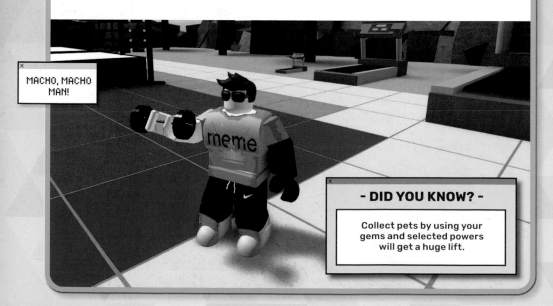

MACHO, MACHO MAN!

- DID YOU KNOW? -

Collect pets by using your gems and selected powers will get a huge lift.

FEEL THE BURN!

HARD WORK PAYS OFF!

A great tip for new stick players is to head over to the tiny zone. This is a special area for players under 500 strength and you can exercise in safety away from taller and bigger gamers. The problem with training in the open is that you're open to attack, as players pick up bonuses for the kills they can make around the map. You can exercise in hidden places, like behind trees, to disguise yourself. Check out the weight bars to beef up your character and bench presses too once they are unlocked.

It's impossible to ignore the gigantic gym dudes who run around the game! These characters have amazing strength and some are super quick too. At this size, you're happy to enter the brawls and take on opponents. Players are invited to brawls and it's best to stay away until you've added some meat and muscle to your frame. So keep an eye on your stats, including height and durability, and aim for as many kills, brawls and rebirths as possible so that you can beat the beefy opponents! Good luck.

25

TREASURE HUNT
SIMULATOR

by **HenryDev**

If we're visiting a beach, we all dream of finding hidden treasure beneath the golden sands. Well, those dreams will come true with Treasure Hunt Simulator! With many similarities to Mining Simulator but with enough twists to make it original, this sim is pure fun and bursting with addictive gameplay.

QUICK STATS

👍 BEST GAMES **RATING: 85%**

VISITS: 335M+   **CREATED:** 19/1/2018   **GENRE:** Simulator

Head to the dig site and start to scratch below the surface and look for buried goodies. The deeper you dig, the higher the value of the prizes you can uncover. Your default backpack has very limited storage, so visit the shop and use your collected coins to use a more effective pack which lets you mine and collect some serious stacks of sand! The standard bucket and spade tools start you off, with shovels being a good upgrade on these. Scoops, rakes and vacuums all carry greater strength under the sand, with

metal detector having 100 strength, but at a cost of 500,000 coins.

Your rank will start to rise as your skills and mining powers do. Be careful not to overstay your welcome in the dig site, though, as there's always a warning sign as to when the ground will collapse! Use the leaderboard to rank the coins, depth, sand and rebirth rates against the best in the game. Lands like Toy, Volcano and Prison can be unlocked once you have the coins in place from your sand digging displays.

x

- DID YOU KNOW? -

The top rank is called yeet, with a mind-boggling 25 billion sand needed to achieve it!

x

FIND THE
TRESURE!

24 GHOST SIMULATOR

by BloxByte Games

To take on this sim, you better not be afraid of ghastly ghosts! Your mission is to search out and destroy the fearsome foes who have taken over the world, using your special equipment alongside your bravery and powers. Up to 12 players can join a server and with 5,000 plus regularly playing at the same time, Ghost Simulator's stats are spooky and spectacular!

QUICK STATS

👍 BEST GAMES RATING: **85%**

VISITS: 61M+   CREATED: 27/12/2018   GENRE: Simulator

Using your fun vacuum sucker, discover the frightening folks, zap them, and use their ectoplasm for your own good! The supernatural substance can be traded for eco tokens and used to buy superior equipment. Upgrade your backpack, too, so that your storage powers are much more effective. Ghosts will dispose of your antenna as well, which is something that you should scoop up as it will allow you to level up and enter even more areas of this sim game!

Some game areas, known as biomes, require special access but you can enter the forest biome first before you target ectoplasm collections. Biomes such as junkyard, sewer, mine, beach and underwater can all follow on. Watch out for limited time events as well – these usually have an extra-scary theme, such as haunted mansion and dinosaur land!

Keep an eye on the boss countdown clock. Bosses are extra scary ghosts with added incentives to defeat them with your super-sucking machines! You have a helpful minimap to guide you in your quests and unlock the rewards you need. With pets and crates also part of Ghost Simulator, you'll have a night full of frights and sights!

ZAP!

ZAP!

- DID YOU KNOW? -

Jump on a hoverboard – it's one of the most fun bits of equipment in Ghost Sim!

SURVIVAL GAMES

Defeating your enemy, beating the obstacles and gaining better items and upgrades – these are all important parts of survival games! The genre can throw many missions your way, from blasting baddies to building quickly or running and climbing to save your life. So keep your eyes open and your brain sharp for this selection of the very best survival games.

FLOOD ESCAPE 2

23

Mix beautifully made obstacle courses with a sense of jeopardy and excitement by playing Flood Escape 2! This massive survival game has clocked 1.5 million favourites and with thousands playing at any one time, there's always a 'flood' of interest around its servers!

As many as 12 gamers can play in an entry-level game. FE2 is an individual adventure, but in reality you rely on your teammates for help and guidance as the pressure cranks up in each level. Enter a zone, such as castle tides (easy) or flood island (normal), and the action begins straight away. Follow the other gamers as you race to press the

by Crazyblox Games

QUICK STATS

👍 BEST GAMES **RATING: 90%**

VISITS: **347M+** CREATED: **13/4/2017** GENRE: **Survival**

- DID YOU KNOW? -

You can practice swimming and diving in lobby area before games.

JUST A HOP, SKIP AND A JUMP!

bright buttons, which in turn will open an exit so you can all progress to the next room. Trouble is, the button will be positioned in a tricky spot and require all the obby (obstacle) game skills that you have in your fingertips! Jump to floating lands, walk along tightropes and skip and bounce to high spots so that you can survive each quest. Work as a team so that you can achieve your goal. Maybe you'll just let the others do the hard work and reach the buttons? However, be warned that you won't be a popular member of the group and also won't collect 10 XP in each game for each button you personally press.

The buttons are easily seen and are lit up from a distance. Often when they are pressed, ladders and bridges will spawn so that each mission can be completed. The jeopardy in FE2 comes with the rising water levels, which will quickly zap your air capacity if you can't escape. Sometimes you need to dive down through an exit tunnel to reach the end – do this quickly otherwise it will be the end game for you! Water is not the only rising danger, though. Acid and lava will also appear, with acid giving you just a few seconds to survive and lava eliminating you instantly. So be brave, quick, skillful and a decent diver and swimmer to make the most of Flood Survival 2!

- DID YOU KNOW? -

There are community-built maps to play in.

CAN YOU MAKE THAT JUMP?

GIANT SURVIVAL

22

Survival skills, shooting, trading and hiding are all essential tactics needed in Giant Survival! Made by the brilliant ROBLOX bods at BIG Games, the guys behind hits like Pet Simulator and BIG Paintball, it's no surprise that this is another massive and mega adventure that can keep you busy for hours!

You don't need to be a master marksman to keep hitting the target in Giant Survival, because the 'person' you're aiming at is so huge anyway! The action begins quickly, although there is an intermission which you can use to select weapons and get

by BIG Games

BEST GAMES RATING: 89%

QUICK STATS

VISITS: 27M+   CREATED: 29/9/2019   GENRE: Survival

- DID YOU KNOW? -

The top weapon is the biochemical blaster, costing a cool 30 million!

HE'S BEHIND YOU!

TEAMWORK!

familiar with the terrain. A random map will spawn, such as castle, tree house, factory or towers, and your task is to shoot and zap the big baddie that appears on the screen! Your weapon will auto aim and as you strike, the money you collect will flash up. This will be one or two bucks at first with low grade weapons, but as you upgrade it can become hundreds each time you make a hit!

The giant's health bar is at the top of the screen. With eight players in the map, you all need to work together to damage and eventually destroy the huge enemy. You can get up close or shoot away from the edge of the map, which means the giant is less likely to capture and kill you! Watch out for the random falling objects around you, such as hot lava rocks or

buildings collapsing. Feel brave and climb buildings to keep up high and reign down chaos on the creature!

Around the map are bright money signs. Scoop these up as you continue to battle and you'll have increased cash to splash in the shop on boosts and gear. Upgrade your weapon as soon as possible, because pistols, miniguns and blasters pack more power than the default crossbow. The giant can be a prisoner, skeleton, ghost or many other scary characters, so work as a group to keep destroying the giant's health bar. Special game modes make it even more of a blast – the triple cash spawn will see your balance rocket up!

BUILD AND SURVIVE

21

BIG Games definitely are a big player in the land of survival games! Here's another cracking and chaotic adventure from the Texas-based developers, packed with quick gameplay and speedy tactics. Get building and survive as long as you can!

by BIG Games

QUICK STATS

👍 BEST GAMES **RATING: 84%**

VISITS: 33M+

CREATED: 10/4/2019

GENRE: Survival

With elements of Minecraft, Fortnite and Zombie Attack, Build and Survive mixes the need to build fortresses and towers with sharp-shooting against the advancing enemies. Before the waves of monsters are unleashed, you have plenty of time to begin building on the ground. You'll start with wood material and the more protective brick and metal can be used when you reach higher levels. You and the other nine players in the server should create powerful towers and buildings to defend you against the robots and zombies. Think about making a thick base, with taller slim towers to give you height. The baddies can attack and punch your buildings, but they can't climb.

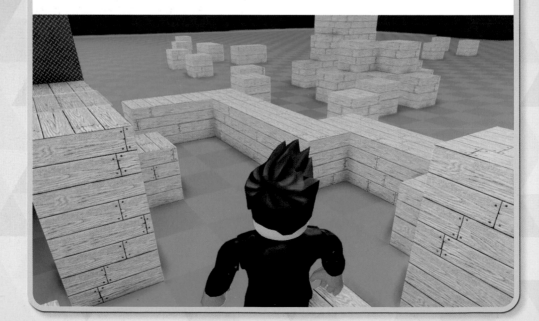

With the weapon you have equipped, fire at the waves as much as possible. You'll earn coins and hearts as a reward and there are stacks of helpful objects to collect around the map – although this puts you at risk of being eliminated! If you get through a round without being killed you'll get a survivor bonus. In the Update 2 in 2019, the premium sun beam was added as a way to harness the power of the sun and unleash deadly beams. Laser beams, cannonballs and lightning strikes are all part of the game as well. Give it a go and you're guaranteed to keep coming back.

- DID YOU KNOW? -

The lowest grade of computer graphics in Build and Survive is called 'potato'. Weird!

I GOT YOU THIS TIME!

YOU'VE GOT GREAT COVER!

SUPER BOMB SURVIVAL

20

Survive the deadly drops from above and plot your way around the room in Super Bomb Survival! As it rockets over 120 million visits and 1.2 million favourites, it's a survival game with much madness and mayhem to offer for individuals and groups of friends.

Gamers can choose from over 100 maps. These include fantastic user-generated scenes from the SBS community, including multiple towers, bases and even pyramids. Vote for your favourite in the lobby and the next round's intensity, on a scale of one to five, will also be revealed. Games typically rank

by Polyhex

QUICK STATS

👍 BEST GAMES **RATING: 84%**

VISITS: 124M+　CREATED: 29/6/2014　GENRE: Survival

- DID YOU KNOW? -

Don't be too down if you lose in the last 30 seconds – you'll get the 'So Close' badge if you do!

WOW!

BOOM!

around 3.5 to 3.7. Before you join the main game, the lobby area is one of the best in ROBLOX! It's rammed with fun activities and is like a minigame in itself. Jump and leap around, hitting coloured buttons, moving giant soccer balls and firing from cannons. Actually, don't miss the chance to launch yourself from a cannon and hit the target as you'll pick up a badge reward!

When the main game is ready and prepared, it's time to join the central room and try to dodge dropping and exploding bombs. Use your unlocked skills, including helicopter-like flying and twists and twirls, to stay safe. Pick up credits and bonuses to unleash new game skills as new jumps and evasive tricks will help you survive the bomb-bastic action. At the end of each game

your scorecard shows the credits collected. Try to collect gems too, as these offer boosts and packs. You can even check out your complete stats – even the 'pizzas eaten' info is shared. Pizzas and bombs? A crazy combo!

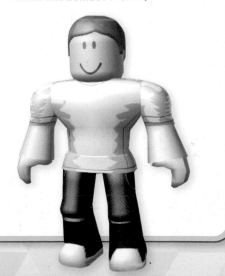

THE FLOOR IS LAVA

19

by TheLegendOfPyro

Ready for some red-hot ROBLOX action? Games don't come much more sizzlin' than The Floor is Lava, where gamers grapple to reach the high ground and stay alive in each round. It's very simple but very addictive, as the 600 million plus visits in less than three years proves!

QUICK STATS

👍 BEST GAMES RATING: **88%**

VISITS:	CREATED:	GENRE:
622M+	15/5/2017	Simulator

In the lobby before the game, use the mini escape games as a way to get your brain in gear before the main match. When you teleport into the map, you have 20 seconds to begin climbing and plotting your path to victory! There are now more than 100 maps to play in, ranging from upside down pyramids to playgrounds, parks and hills. When the countdown clock finishes, race to reach the highest spot you can see as the lethal lava begins to rise and cause panic. New players should take tips from experienced people around them, copying the routes they take and the jumps and leaps they make. Your obby game skills will need to be in top shape, as one wrong move could see you fall and be destroyed in the hot liquid! You have a few seconds to survive in the lava, so move quickly if you enter it.

As you collect points for successful survivals, trade in for items like gravity and speed coils, armour and hooks. These will help climb and survive and if you're flush with Robux, game passes can reward you with jetpacks and flying clouds!

FIND THE HIGH GROUND!

- DID YOU KNOW? -

You can even try jumping and standing on players' heads!

NATURAL DISASTER
SURVIVAL

by **Stickmasterluke**

Think fast and avoid the incoming danger as you play Natural Disaster Survival! Your mission is to act in the best way to tackle the problem that's about to sweep your map, ranging from earthquakes to volcanic eruptions and acid rain. It's a dangerous world out there, people!

QUICK STATS

👍 BEST GAMES **RATING: 91%**

VISITS:	CREATED:	GENRE:
1B+	28/3/2008	Survival

From the lobby tower, a random map is selected for each match, which could be the raceway track, amusement park or palace. After teleporting there, you have about 20 seconds before the incoming disaster details are given out. Use the given instructions to cope with the disaster, which may be a sandstorm, blizzard, tsunami or flash flood. A lot of the time this will mean climbing to a safe ground, such as in a flood, but don't always climb to the very highest point. Some very tall structures may become unstable and collapse resulting in fall damage. Mistakes players make are to always scramble for a high position without knowing what the natural disaster will be.

Have a look up at the sky to try to work out what the approaching natural force will be. If the air turns yellow and misty, it means a sandstorm is coming and you'll want to be sheltering inside a secure building. Pick up rewards such as balloons that help you rise to safety, and game passes which give you some great in-game boosts, like the compass and VIP privileges.

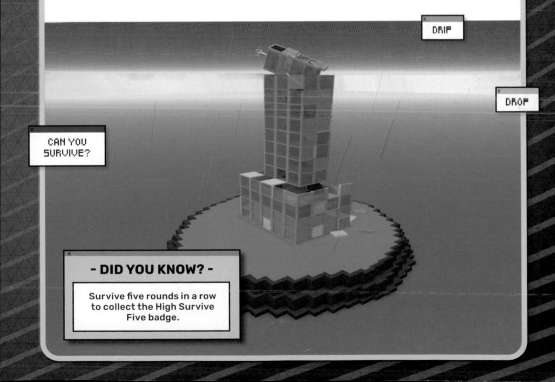

DRIP

DROP

CAN YOU SURVIVE?

- DID YOU KNOW? -

Survive five rounds in a row to collect the High Survive Five badge.

BUILDING

Putting blocks on blocks and creating big or small structures, building games are much more than just a construction craze! Often you need to build to survive or to defeat an enemy, or you could be creating stuff to make loads of cash. Builds can be from your imagination or using set plans, and the following eight games show what the popular genre is all about!

BUILDING SIMULATOR

17

Build and build and build and build... this game is all about, yep you've guessed it, BUILDING! For a sim-style title there's no real roleplaying going on, as this fast-growing game focuses on putting up speedy structures in a simple way on a simple map. Built by Just For Fun, Building Simulator does exactly that!

The purpose is to construct buildings and objects from pre-fabricated plans, called blueprints. The map is always the same and is just a vast green space, so there's plenty of room for all users to be creative in, with a maximum of seven players allowed together. The first thing that can be built are trees, which are unlocked from the beginning and give you

by Just For Fun

QUICK STATS

BEST GAMES RATING: **89%**

VISITS: 45M+

CREATED: 6/3/2019

GENRE: Building

- DID YOU KNOW? -

Building Simulator 2 was also released by the same developers in November 2019.

THIS ONE'S MINE!

a value of $5. Keep building this to increase your cash to $530, because then you can unlock the whole object and begin to see some bigger cash flow to your bank account! You shouldn't just focus on creating bigger buildings.

Equipping more efficient tools is a smart move. The default stick is slow to work, with stone carrying 1.5x more power at a cost of $220. Aim for something like the wrench, at $15,500 and with 1,100 times more power than the stick, to really give your building a massive help! Always be weighing up the value of saving for new blueprints against the benefit that better tools bring.

The tank, ROBLOX sign, tower, complex and classic house have a reward value of between $2,270 and $88.2 million, so there's a vast range of construction options available. Pick up some helpers to follow you around the map and take care of your building for you so that you can focus on establishing your empire.

The rebirthing option is a big tactic in your Build Sim abilities. For a basic cost of $2,250, it allows you to triple the value of your builds and turn them gold, which really sets you out as a decorative player that belongs among the best! It is worth noting that production also goes up by 50% during rebirth.

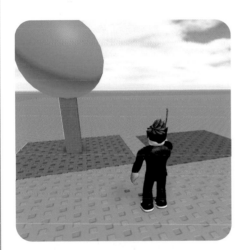

16 RETAIL TYCOON

Yep, it has 'tycoon' in the title, but this game is as much about brilliant building as it is about making stacks of cash! Retail Tycoon is a great combination of creating an environment that you want to do business in and role-play action, where customers arrive to take advantage of the buildings and scenes you've put in place.

Retail Tycoon is a very structured game, with all the options and selections you can make to build clearly marked out before you in the 'build' area. When the game spawns, players claim 5,000 cash as soon as they claim a vacant piece of land and then go to build up their retail establishment. The first thing to build is a display item, such as a shelf,

by Haggie125

QUICK STATS

👍 BEST GAMES RATING: **90%**

VISITS: **183M+** CREATED: **14/8/2015** GENRE: **Building**

freezer or display table. These can then be stocked with appropriate goods, such as food, toys or books from the 'supply' tab. You may need to employ workers too and once you start selling goods, your cash flow will increase and boost the building options you have. If you find that you no longer need an item, such as a shelf, storage racks or office desk, these can be sold back for 80% of their original value.

x WHAT SHALL I CHOOSE?

THIS WILL BE MY SHOP!

With money coming into your retail building, you can begin to look at bigger building plans and details. Walls, flooring and ceiling can be detailed to your own taste and, if you change your mind once they are added, you have the option to bulldoze them and reclaim half of their cost! The upgrade tab has some of the grandest building options for gamers. Land can be purchased around your base, ranging from 1,000 to 5,000 per patch, and the parking lot can be made more attractive and bigger, too. This will set you back between 1,000 to 25,000, which is a costly thing!

Every aspect of the building devices in Retail Tycoon needs to be geared towards helping you to make more money, so think carefully before starting any grand expansion plans as you always need the money in the bank to pay for it!

- DID YOU KNOW? -

Robbers will try to enter your building, so be quick to stop them if they do!

HOMEBUILDER

by **madattak**

For the simple joy of building in a relaxed and timeless setting, few games can match HomeBuilder! And with so many options and inspiring ways to make you think, you can set about making the home of your dreams. Just don't turn it into a nightmare by messing up your building plans!

QUICK STATS

👍 **BEST GAMES RATING: 83%**

VISITS: 1M+   **CREATED:** 4/5/2017   **GENRE:** Building

Enter the vast map and the world is yours to build on. Go to the plot tab on your screen and select your baseplate from four settings – grass, sand, tarmac or concrete. The plot is then yours to add to from a long list of building choices. Starting with the basics is a good choice, and perhaps you'll place some trees and shrubs around the edge of your land? There are six plants to pick from and you can also turf an area if you like. When you begin to design and form structures, choose whether you want a historical or modern appearance and what type

of walls, doors and features it will have. Don't worry if you create something you quickly don't like, because the 'clear baseplate' button quickly wipes the plot clean for a fresh slate to start creating on again.

Inside your buildings you can start to add a personal touch. Furniture items include chairs, beds, sofas and storage units, as well as books, toasters and presents for a really cute look! For some cool products, like executive dining sets, flat screen TVs and laptops, you'll need to use Robux, but there's still plenty to pick from for free. Save your work in one of nine slots and get creative again the next time to drop by.

- DID YOU KNOW? -

There's a helpful tutorial session to give you the building basics!

COME BY FOR DINNER SOME TIME!

DESIGN IT!

14

by **tktech**

Building games don't have to be just about building gigantic houses, towers and city landscapes! Building can also mean small scale stuff, like creating your own... human! Design It! is a bit like that, as the aim is to build a cool look for your avatar for a certain theme and then other gamers get to vote if they like it. If you're a building fan, give this quirky and quick game a go!

Join a server (maximum of eight players) and you're told to design an avatar to match the round's chosen theme. Themes can be vast and varied, from gym star to teenager, sport to space and animals to robots! Importantly, you can only build a look using the budget you have, which won't be much at first. Scroll through the options and you'll find tools and objects for every part of your character, from hair and headwear

QUICK STATS

👍 BEST GAMES **RATING: 89%**

VISITS:	CREATED:	GENRE:
212M+	15/4/2016	Building

to coloured trousers. The function is much like the regular avatar editor in the ROBLOX home page, so you'll be familiar with how to operate it.

Keep that theme's round in mind and build the most eye-catching look possible. Body style, avatar type, effects and even pets can be added! Submit your design, then wait for the show to start. All designs will line up and this is your chance to vote for your favourite outfit – sadly you can't vote for yourself! The winners will be revealed from behind the red curtain and after the round results, cash will be awarded so that your budget is boosted. Good luck, folks!

IMAGINE IT – DESIGN IT!

DESIGN IT!

WELCOME TO ROBLOX BUILDING

13

by CloneTrooper1019

This is one for the builders out there! If a construction fan wants a fun and relaxing session of simple building with no pressure from other users or enemies, then load up this unique title and you'll be happy for hours or even days!

QUICK STATS

👍 BEST GAMES **RATING: 87%**

VISITS:	CREATED:	GENRE:
5M+	25/2/2019	Building

Previous versions of a game like this existed in the early years of ROBLOX, but then became broken or outdated, which was a big shame for the building community. So CloneTrooper1019, inspired by the original creators such as Stickmasterluke, HotThoth and darthskrill, set about bringing it back. By spring 2020, Welcome to ROBLOX Building (WTRB) was a cool game with more features, blocks and customization than anything else like it before!

Start by claiming a baseplate and let your building imagination go to town! The setting for the builds is like a Lego baseplate on the floor of a lounge in a house, which is really fun. Usually there will be some epic builds around by other players to check out too. Have a good explore around and get some ideas – you might see houses, towers and even cars and playgrounds. If you see something you like, just give it a 'like' and the creator will be delighted!

They have every type of set and kit you can imagine, from basic to advanced kits and building for houses, castles and also space-themed creations. There are also machines, wiring elements and even Christmas and Halloween props. Grab your stamper tool and get creative!

SO MANY OPTIONS!

12

BUILD A BOAT
FOR TREASURE

by Chillz Studios

Well, the name of this game says it all to be honest... nothing else needs to be added! Okay, let's give you some super stats and facts about this simple but slick and stylish building game! With well over 600 million views and frequently more than 20,000 concurrent players, Build a Boat for Treasure keeps racking up the numbers that makes it one of the best of all time in the genre.

QUICK STATS

BEST GAMES **RATING:** **85%**

VISITS: 626M+

CREATED: 2/11//2016

GENRE: Building

In the huge build area at the water's edge, this is your space to craft a boat. At first you will just have a small amount of wooden blocks and a seat, so any vessel you create is very basic but will still float on the water – it won't look much like a boat, though! For beginner builders, it will probably take several attempts after you launch your ship to become familiar with navigating the water and getting past the rocks and obstacles in the way.

In Build a Boat for Treasure, the aim is to get your boat through each challenge by sailing a path through the water. You'll learn how builds automatically move past rocks, plus understand how they can get stuck and what it takes to be a successful boat builder. Each time you do get through a level you can pick up gold and treasure rewards, which will help you construct bigger and more impressive ships. Remember, though, that the largest vessels are not automatically the best!

There's a lot to learn and take in, but if you just love crafting, designing and colouring big objects, this boat-based adventure is definitely for you!

MY BOAT, MY RULES!

- DID YOU KNOW? -

It can be played in single or team mode.

BUILD BATTLE

11

by **P& J Studios**

Don't worry – there's not actually any fighting involved in Build Battle! It's all about construction and being imaginative with the tools you have. Ultimately, you're competing to be the best against the other builders. Let the build battle commence!

QUICK STATS

👍 BEST GAMES **RATING: 85%**

VISITS: 16M+ **CREATED:** 30/6/2017 **GENRE:** Building

Made by the uber talented developing and scripting trio of TheLegendOfPyro, SummerEquinox and EncodedLua, Build Battle puts up to eight players in a server against each other and challenges you to create the best build that you can in the allotted time. A random theme is selected, ranging from aliens and castles to sports to history, and builders must create a structure to fit this. Themes can be bought for 25 Robux and when the round begins, use the tools and materials to scope out a design that you think will impress the other users!

This could be anything from a building, to an arrangement that looks like an animal, or any other feature that relates to the topic. Use colours and techniques that will stand out from the rest. When the time's up, each player then has a chance to rate each building, using the five emoji buttons at the bottom of the screen. The overall winner is revealed and the game results ranked – you don't want to be at the bottom of the league! Credits are awarded for success, which means you can then use better materials and items in future rounds. May the best builder win!

x
- DID YOU KNOW? -

The speedy red and blue tracks take you round the edge of the build area to view all of the creations!

x
3... 2... 1
BUILD!

10 PLANE CRAZY

by **madattak**

Originally developed by madattak several years ago before being taken up and pushed further by rickje139, Plane Crazy is full of interesting building features with strong design and scientific elements too. It's a fun game, but it may take a while to get up to speed with, so hang in there, building buddies!

	QUICK STATS		
👍	**BEST GAMES RATING:**	**85%**	
	VISITS: 26M+	**CREATED:** 16/7/2014	**GENRE:** Building

There are not many successful plane-inspired games in ROBLOX, and certainly not those that let you build and create your own set of wicked winged machines. From the basic blocks, beams, wedges, wings and cylinders that you have, your task is to create a plane in your build zone and then put it to test down the runway. Cool! Don't be put off by the technical talk, though. The orange build icon is where to begin, as this opens the materials you need. Guidelines show how to lay the pieces so the plane's centre of mass is correct. Add fuel blocks from the propulsions tab, along with wings, wheels and everything else.

Don't forget to select your engine! Choose between jet and rocket power as the way to get your plane off the tarmac and when you're done building, click the green plane button to start testing! The physics, components and colours can all be fine-tuned and fiddled with too. Take a look at other designs on the runway and if you have chat enabled, ask other experienced builders for any tips. Enjoy the Plane Crazy journey!

- DID YOU KNOW? -

There's a helpful tutorial session to give you the building basics!

COME FLY WITH ME!

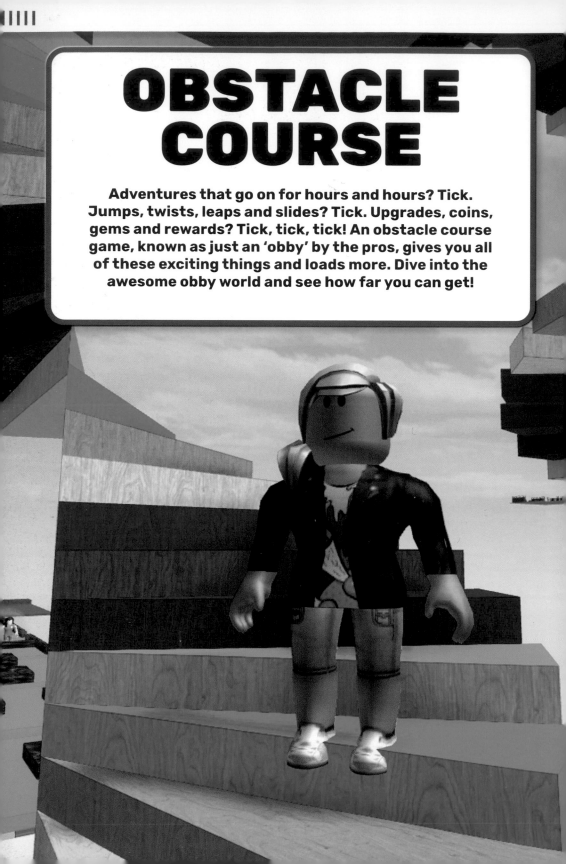

OBSTACLE COURSE

Adventures that go on for hours and hours? Tick.
Jumps, twists, leaps and slides? Tick. Upgrades, coins,
gems and rewards? Tick, tick, tick! An obstacle course
game, known as just an 'obby' by the pros, gives you all
of these exciting things and loads more. Dive into the
awesome obby world and see how far you can get!

MEGA FUN
OBBY

09

With over 2,000 stages, it's easy to see why Bloxtun calls Mega Fun Obby the most fun obstacle course in the world! It's also probably the biggest, so users can easily spend hours leaping and racing around this utterly epic course in the sky!

Spawn in the game and you're off straight away. Mega Fun Obby can be enjoyed as an individual or played with a friend, and lots of people enjoy racing to see who can finish each level the quickest. But with so many levels, it can be a long race! You will be jumping on discs, squares and cylinders every split second. Each time you reach a white pad marks a respawn point, so when you fall off (which you will!) you're not taken all the way back to the start. Phew!

by Schwifty Studios

QUICK STATS

BEST GAMES
RATING: 90%

VISITS: 945M+

CREATED: 10/7/2009

GENRE: Adventure

- DID YOU KNOW? -

If you love Mega Fun Obby, check out Mega Fun Obby 2 as well!

ONE STEP AT A TIME!

Collecting Mega Loyalty Points (MLP) is important in the game. Collect as many as possible as these rewards can be used to buy items and boosts in the shops. Cool gear such as speedy shoes, gravity balloons, flying carpets and coils will have you flying forward around the course and cutting down on your finishing time. Another major bonus in Mega Fun Obby is the skip function. This allows you to miss out a level, but after you've used your free one you'll need to buy another or earn them as rewards.

Fast passes are mini cheats which can be bought. They allow you to skip forward stages, but they can be very expensive – jumping to stage 1,700 costs a mighty 18,000 Robux! Pets also give you some friendship as you bounce around the endless areas of the obby map, as well as giving a big boost to your gameplay. Pets come at different tiers and along with the rebirth tool can really liven up your awesome obby experience! The global leaderboard ranks the game's very best players from pets collected, game session length and total rebirths. Keep practicing and maybe one day your name will appear!

08 OBSTACLE PARADISE

by I-C-T Studios

This is a **ROBLOX game that lets you build your own obstacle course AND play those built by others** – awesome! It's a must-visit place for fans of the genre and with easy-play functions, gamers can stick around for a long time as they dream up their own attraction and have fun cruising and jumping around up to seven others!

QUICK STATS

BEST GAMES **RATING: 83%**

VISITS: 42M+
CREATED: 22/1/2017
GENRE: Adventure

Eight players in total can join a server and your first task is to claim an unused obby area as your own. Look at the red cash box on your screen – this begins at awarding you $5 every five seconds. The total cash that you have is what allows you to buy items for your obby, from the build tab. Have a look around the other creations that players have constructed for some ideas, and to have some fun as well of course! Your own personal style can be added to your attraction.

There's loads to choose from in the build function. Lava floors, parkour obstacles and essentials such as twists, turns, win buttons and stairs are all there. Don't worry that if you fall off your obby you have to complete it all again to reach the end – just click the 'teleport to end' button and you'll instantly appear there! Dive into the store and gear, cash and perks can all be selected and the upgrade area is vital, too. Here you can boost the income, interval and obby length settings (if you can afford them) to make your experience even more fun.

- DID YOU KNOW? -

At $550, the reverse lava wall conveyor is an epic obstacle item!

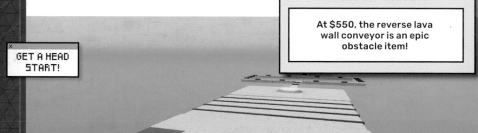

GET A HEAD START!

ESCAPE THE SCHOOL OBBY

07

by NICKGAME54 Fan Group

Obby games don't need to be endless adventures with gazillions of levels and courses that can drive you crazy! This game keeps you busy for long enough, perhaps around six or seven minutes when you're very experienced, but could take over an hour for newcomers. Plus, who doesn't want to escape from school every now and then!

QUICK STATS

👍 BEST GAMES **RATING: 86%**

VISITS: 108 M+ | CREATED: 22/8/2018 | GENRE: All Genres

The action begins in the classroom. Your helpful (but scary looking!) guide tells you to get out of the room as the teacher is about to go a bit berserk! Leave through the door and the quest is on. Obstacles such as giant pencils, fallen lockers and burst water pipes in the hallways need to be navigated. Head for the spawn button with a face printed on it at the end of each level to secure your route around the course. You might think you've reached a dead end at times, with no doors you're able to pass through. When this happens, simply take a look up and escape through the vents in the walls!

The gruesome guides can also give you some tests, like choosing the right path to take across a problem – pick the wrong one and you'll be wiped out! Escape the School Obby can also give you tricky questions to answer and you will need to pass through the right answer in order to proceed. Don't go getting stuck in the vent maze for too long or else you'll never get to finish the course and reach the schoolyard!

- DID YOU KNOW? -

In the messy school canteen there are manky pizza slices chucked on the ground!

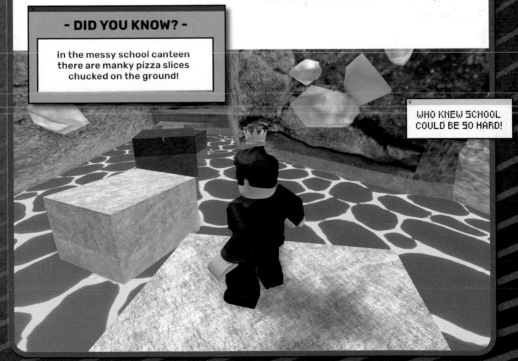

WHO KNEW SCHOOL COULD BE SO HARD!

PUZZLES

Challenge yourself and take on a ROBLOX puzzle game! There are plenty to choose from and they offer a variety of tests and missions, from quick quizzes and quests to more fancy obby-like challenges that need thought and time. Search through the Games page for your faves, and here are some that puzzle fans enjoy taking on!

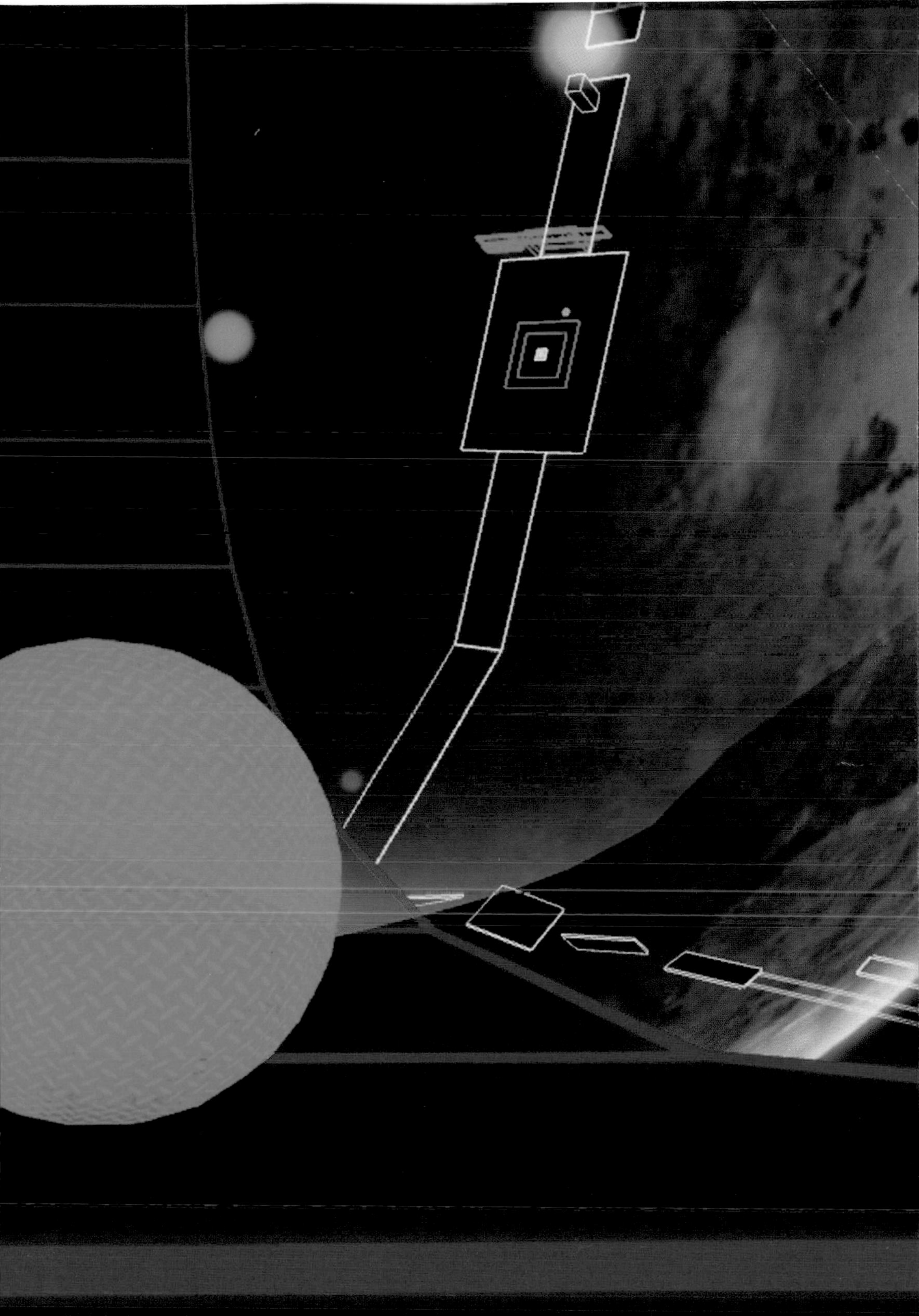

ESCAPE ROOM SIMULATOR

06

by DevUltra

When **ROBLOX** officially say a game is tough to beat, then that's proof you'll need to be smart and use some quick thinking to progress through the levels! This hugely popular puzzle game, made by the clever people at DevUltra, requires a sharp and skillful brain to escape each room. Keep your eyes open for any clues!

Players can take on escape room quests as a solo player or in a team. The choice at the beginning is to enter the starter pack. The adventurer pack, challenger pack and explorer pack will come later once you have earned keys from the rooms and leveled up. Or, if you're lucky enough to have Robux, packs can be purchased. Enter the starter pack and choose from the prison break, treasure cave or I hate Mondays routes. Wherever you go, just keep an open mind – don't

QUICK STATS

👍 BEST GAMES **RATING: 89%**

VISITS: 62M+ | CREATED: 21/3/2017 | GENRE: Adventure

- DID YOU KNOW? -

In the lobby, the game shows off its Bloxy award for Hardest Game!

NOW HOW DO I GET OUT OF HERE?

believe that anything you see is as straight forward as it appears!

Clues are everywhere in the rooms, and anything that looks slightly unusual or out of place is worth investigating closely. Try clicking on objects, such as bookcases or tables, to reveal any hidden hints that may help you. Furniture may move so that you can progress through each task and always look up as well as down. Keys may be hanging high and you'll need a long object to reach them.

Characters can level up with their keys or use any spare cash in the escape room store. The in-game currency is called escape coins. Another great feature is that maps can be created by the Escape Room community, and submitted for possible inclusion in the game. There's also an option to create a party with friends, which is easily set up via the joint party menu facility.

Each room has to be cracked before the time runs out, so there's no option to relax and wait around for ages and hope that a brainwave hits you! Before each quest, the time allowed is clearly displayed, along with the difficulty level of the room. The store offers extras such as cosmetics and boosts, and there are even bundles loaded with keys and coins to help speed you along.

MAKE SURE YOU KEEP AN EYE OUT FOR CLUES!

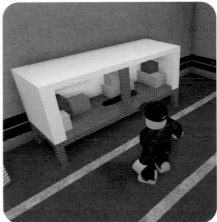

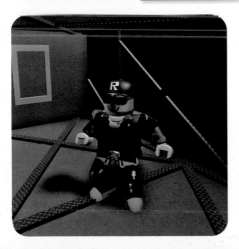

GU**ESS** TH**E** DRAWING!

by GFSFF

This puzzle game will 'draw' on all your talent and experience! Titles in this genre can be a complete quiz fest, packed with challenges, head scratchers and real brain bogglers. But this easy game is so simple, so fun and so addictive!

QUICK STATS

👍 BEST GAMES RATING: **87%**

VISITS: 10M+   **CREATED:** 9/6/2019   **GENRE:** All Genres

Jump into the action along with six other ROBLOXIANS and your task will be to draw something on the giant board ahead of you. The other gamers then have to guess what you're creating, so make sure you do a good job and help the others with good detail! You'll have to wait your turn to draw, which means you'll compete against the rest to be the first to successfully work out what the mystery item and word is. There's the chance to type your guess on the screen – spell the word correctly, too! Once the clock has ticked down and the word is revealed, the points for that round will then flash up.

Points are awarded for how quickly you guessed the word, which may range from over 150 points to around just 30 – or zero if you don't guess correctly! The overall leaderboard displays the top points winners as well as the guesses they have used. Don't be fooled into thinking this is just a quick drawing contest – it's a real competition!

There are shortcuts you can take, such as revealing a hint for the guess word and jumping the queue to get your turn quicker, but these cost Robux.

The word is:

Reveal hint

GRAVITY SHIFT

by **meguy1**

Science, action, skills... this puzzle game is stuffed with so many exciting aspects! Compared to other quiz or strategy-based titles, Gravity Shift is different and you need lots of practice and patience to complete the various levels. It's still a puzzling game to master, though!

QUICK STATS

BEST GAMES **RATING: 83%**

VISITS: 44M+   **CREATED:** 18/4/2012   **GENRE:** All Genres

Set in a far off galaxy with a strong space theme, your mission is to move a small ball through a course and guide it to checkpoints and end zones. There is a big dose of obstacle course about it and the difficulty levels rise the further you get. The routes don't stay flat, though, like other obby games. You'll be turned upside down and twisted around and must keep the ball on the path as you do. Whether you're playing on a keyboard, tablet or console, you must get a quick grip of the controls and functions to last the course!

The levels include beginner's jumps, stairs, right angles, curve-tastic, strafe the angles and crazy jumps. You have the option to automatically teleport to the tasks you've completed, just in case your ball does fall away. Upgrades such as custom colours make you look super cool and the double jump ball allows you to really stand out from the crowd, too. Your total time on each level is recorded and this will be compared to the time taken against the previous level. So, complete each one as quickly and as safely as you can.

- DID YOU KNOW? -

You can see Earth in the background as you play Gravity Shift's puzzle levels!

KEEP PRACTICING!

MINIGAMES

If you're looking for a big buzz of crazy games and quick-fire action, playing minigames is perfect for you! This genre is packed with options, offering all sorts of inventive and unique activities with the ultimate aim of surviving, progressing and bossing your opponents. Pick up coins, items and upgrades to boost your experience and success rate.

03 EPIC MINIGAMES

'Epic' is the only way to describe this huge ROBLOX adventure! With over 90 unique and exciting games by spring 2020, and with new maps added all the time, gamers are treated to a monster range of sick challenges to enjoy as a solo player or with friends in a group.

by TypicalType

QUICK STATS

BEST GAMES RATING: **90%**

VISITS: 962M+
CREATED: 29/7/2015
GENRE: All Genres

The lobby area in Epic Minigames is big and impressive, too. There's lots of cool information and details on display, including the current minigame and voting for the next game, and as the countdown starts to the upcoming game you can even have a quick swim in the sea! When games spawn, you have a few seconds to prepare for the test and instructions always appear at the top of the screen, telling you what to do.

Try to watch what others do, as they may be more experienced than you.

The choice of quick-fire games can include jumping, climbing, dodging things and escaping. Games usually last between 60 to 90 seconds and the settings can vary from intergalactic zones to snowy mountains, spinning wheels, monsters and playgrounds. Try to survive right until the end for added bonuses!

BOUNCE! BOUNCE!

Gamers are rewarded with coins which can be used to get boosts from gear and passes, plus cosmetic improvements from effects and pets. Leveling up is a big incentive to achieve success in the minigames. Your on-screen info will reveal how many game wins you need to go up a level. Daily missions are also listed, which could target a victory in solo or team modes, or something such as success in a controller minigame. Purchasing a VIP pass with Robux will get you going on the VIP mission quests.

Get onto the pro servers as soon as possible by using Robux or by reaching level 24. The pro server rewards you with x1.5 coin collection and increased challenges. Level badges are unlocked from level 4 onwards for the minigamer honour, extending to medals including control freak, champion and quick escape for much higher tiers.

RIPULL MINIGAMES

02

by **Ripull**

Minigame games may all look a bit familiar, offering a selection of fun activities and rewards for doing well, but Ripull Minigames carries off its own distinctive look and feel. It's definitely worth playing regularly alongside the genre-leading Epic Minigames!

QUICK STATS

BEST GAMES
RATING: 82%

VISITS:	CREATED:	GENRE:
274M+	20/9/2014	Comedy

Ripull Minigames has much less games to offer and isn't updated as frequently as some, but don't let that put you off. The games are really well made, with good graphics and large maps. The selection ranges from crazy mazes, speed runs, bomb battles, plane attacks and frozen battles against snowy characters – all awesome fun! The length of games can change and generally you need to survive until the end in order to collect stacks of Ripull coins, which is the game's currency. Gems, another reward system, are also dished out and these can be collected by spending Robux too.

The lobby is just as good as Epic Minigames, with fun features like trampolines, diving boards, floating blocks, oversized balls and underground caves to keep you busy while the clock counts down to the next game. In the intermission, use your time to pick up extras like pets, pods and game boosts. The +15 speed, +30 jump power and crate luck boost features are well worth shopping for, as is the +150% experience boost button. If you want to play as a team or with friends, the squads option is brilliant. Up to eight players can join a squad and points are pooled together, with a squad leader taking charge of the group!

- DID YOU KNOW? -

x

Ripull Minigames was originally called Minigame Madness!

x

YOU CAN EQUIP 3 TOYS FOR FREE!

MINI GOLF

by **Widgeon**

A great way to mix minigames with the tricky sport of golf! Mini Golf has a stash of cool courses to play, against as many as 11 other opponents. All you need is a steady aim and to apply the right power to your club to place your ball in the hole. Sounds simple? It can be, but it can also be frustrating!

QUICK STATS

BEST GAMES
RATING: **85%**

VISITS: 5.5 M+
CREATED: 9/1/2015
GENRE: Adventure

There are more than 90 mini courses to play through in this laidback adventure title. In the first person mode, you see your ball at the beginning of the hole and must carefully line up the power gauge in a way that will see it move towards the hole in the most efficient way. The par rating means how many shots you should take to hole the ball. Take more shots than the par rating and you'll get fewer points at the end. Finish under par for a bigger boost to your score.

The mini courses vary in difficulty. There will be lots of twists and turns, secret tunnels, hills, obstacles, mazes and more. Navigating your ball through each challenge is not always easy! At the beginning of each play, you are shown a quick view of the whole course, so use this to work out your strategy. Also, let other gamers go first so that you can see how their shots react to the surface and challenges. Don't always use max power, as your ball could go out of bounds and you'll have to start again!

- DID YOU KNOW? -

Don't take too long because each hole is against the clock!

YOU CAN EVEN CUSTOMISE YOUR FAVOURITE GOLF BALL!

HOLE IN ONE!

ROBLOX BRAIN BUSTERS!

Now that you're a ROBLOX gaming guru, it's time to take on the ultimate test! Enjoy this fun quiz – all the questions are based on what you've read from this book!

Find the **answers** on page **192**.

1 **Which of these is not a ROBLOX game genre?**

A. Horror

B. Western

C. Karaoke

2 **In which year was Mad City created?**

A. 2008

B. 2017

C. 2019

3 **What is the term 'sim' short for in ROBLOX?**

A. Simulator
B. Simon Says
C. Simples

4 **Which of these games has over 1 billion visits?**

A. Full Throttle
B. Super Hero Tycoon
C. Flood Escape 2

5 **Pick the real ROBLOX developer from this list...**

A. REE-create
B. Rub_bish Games
C. BIG Games

6 **When you wait for a game to start, what is this often called?**

A. Intermission
B. Interval
C. Inter Milan

7 **Which of these is ROBLOX not officially playable on?**

A. Nintendo Switch
B. Tablet
C. PlayStation

8 **What is the official currency of ROBLOX?**

A. Dollars
B. Robux
C. Buxro

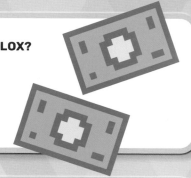

9 **What is the obstacle game genre better known as?**

A. Obs
B. Obby
C. Jumpy leapy

10 **Which of these is an option when creating an avatar?**

A. R15
B. R2-D2
C. Toys R Us

11 **What does RPG mean?**

A. Role playing game
B. Real playing game
C. Reactive player game

12 **When a game has lots of places to play in, what are these often called?**

A. Atlases
B. Globes
C. Maps

13 **What are games involving cash, businesses and customers known as?**

A. Executive
B. Tycoon
C. Finance

14 **Which of these is a genuine part of building games?**

A. Base cement
B. Base ground
C. Baseplate

15 Can you name the massively popular hiding game?

A. Extreme Hide and Seek
B. Hide and Seek Extreme
C. Seek and Hide to Extreme

16 Which of these games has more than 3 billion visits?

A. Arsenal
B. Ninja Legends
C. Jailbreak

17 Who is the skillful developer behind the massive MeepCity game?

A. Dued1
B. alexnewtron
C. Badimo

18 Getting a new look for a weapon or item is usually called a...

A. Skin
B. Surface
C. Jacket

19   What is a type of reward picked up in lots of games?

A. PvP
B. XP
C. Peas

20   In the Build and Survive game, which of these is a real gameplay term?

A. Parsnip
B. Turnip
C. Potato

21   Which of these devices can give you simple game tips and advice?

A. A tutorial
B. A teacher
C. A telephone

22   A first person shooter where you aim to be the final survivor is called what type of game?

A. Final royale
B. Battle royale
C. Royale wedding

23 What is the phrase when you can instantly appear or move to a new area?

A. Vanish

B. Switch

C. Teleport

24 When a game hasn't been fully released or finished testing, what is this called?

A. BETA

B. BEE

C. BLOOM

25 What is not a real job in Work at a Pizza Place?

A. Cashier

B. Cook

C. Cleaner

26 Which of these is a type of upgrading in a game?

A. Rewind

B. Rebirth

C. Retake

27 What are the materials called in Mining Simulator?

A. Ores

B. Solids

C. Beans

28 From the home page, where are things like accessories, emotes and shirts accessed?

A. Groups

B. Inventory

C. Blog

29 Complete the missing word from this game title: Escape the _ _ _ _ _ _ Obby.

A. School

B. Police

C. Monster

30 What type of creature attacks in a mega game created by Horror Portals?

A. Ghost

B. Vampire

C. Zombie

GAMING GLOSSARY

AFK
This stands for "away from keyboard". It can be typed in chat to let others know that you're not currently active, or used to identify an unresponsive enemy target.

AVATAR
Your character in ROBLOX is called your avatar. It can be customized with clothes and effects and edited to look different to other avatars.

BADGE
Badges are given out during games depending on success and victories. They are a great incentive to progress and do well, with some being very hard to achieve.

BLOXY
The Bloxy awards are the official ROBLOX medals given to game creators. The ceremony takes place each year and developers are desperate to win one!

CODES
Most games offer codes, which can be typed in during play to achieve a new skill, upgrade or boost. Codes can be revealed on screen and often through social media.

CONCURRENT
Meaning "at the same time." Devs and game creators talk about concurrent players on their titles and the amount of traffic and users that a server can handle.

DEV
Short for developer. A game's developer is the person who builds a game, often helped by a bigger team and with scripters and editors.

GEAR
For gamers, it's a general in-game term used for things like items, clothes, weapons, tools and machines that are needed for success or that a player has for use in the future.

GLITCH
A temporary problem in a game, such as a function not working or a cheat being enabled. Glitches can be reported and fixed by the developer.

GUI
Graphical user interface. It describes how a player connects with a game through the pictures, videos, buttons and icons it displays. The best always have a GUI that's easy to understand.

LTM

Limited time mode. This can be a game mode that's available for a short time or an event or special occasion that will expire. LTMs often create a lot of excitement in gaming communities.

NPC

Non-playable character. These are automated players that appear in a game, either as enemies or characters that interact with you. Often called bots or robots.

OP

This means "over-powered" and is a phrase gamers use to describe a weapon, item or function that is too powerful for a game and negatively disrupts the flow.

ROBLOXIAN

Avatars can also be known as Robloxians. Experienced players often use this word. ROBLOXIA is the ROBLOX universe in general.

ROBUX

The in-game currency for ROBLOX. With the help of an adult, a Robux account can be set up and must be paid for with real money. Robux can be used to purchase cosmetics, boosts, perks and more.

RTHRO

Released in 2018, Rthro is a realistic body part and movement system for avatars. It is a development on the R15 and R6 character types.

SPAWN

The point where you begin, or appear, in a game. Re-spawn points can be used further into a game to save going back to the beginning. Enemies and items can also spawn at random.

STUDIO

The ROBLOX Studio is the place that anyone can build, create and develop their own games. Use templates, themes and toolbox items to set up a fun setting.

VIP

Very important person. VIPs can relate to special invite-only games, restricted access servers and game passes which offer shortcuts and boosts.

VR

This means "virtual reality". Some ROBLOX games and systems support VR equipment, with headsets. Here environments appear super life-like to the users.

ROBLOX BRAIN BUSTERS!
ANSWERS

1. C; **2.** B; **3.** A; **4.** B; **5.** C; **6.** A; **7.** C;

8. B; **9.** A; **10.** A; **11.** A; **12.** C; **13.** B; **14.** C; **15.** E; **16.** C; **17.** B; **18.** A;

19. B; **20.** C; **21.** A; **22.** B; **23.** C;

24. A; **25.** C; **26.** B; **27.** A;

28. B; **29.** A; **30.** C;

HOW DID *YOU* DO?